Multimodal Discourse

Multimodal Discourse

The modes and media of contemporary communication

GUNTHER KRESS
Culture, Communication and Societies,
Institute of Education, University of London

THEO VAN LEEUWEN
Centre for Language and Communication Research,
Cardiff University

Bloomsbury Academic India
An imprint of Bloomsbury Publishing Plc

BLOOMSBURY
NEW DELHI • LONDON • OXFORD • NEW YORK • SYDNEY

BLOOMSBURY INDIA
Bloomsbury Publishing India Pvt. Ltd
Second Floor, LSC Building No. 4, DDA Complex, Pocket C-6&7,
Vasant Kunj, New Delhi 110070

BLOOMSBURY, Bloomsbury Academic India and the Diana
logo are trademarks of Bloomsbury Publishing Plc

First published in 2001 by Hodder Education, part of Hachette UK
Reprinted by Bloomsbury Academic 2017
First published in India 2022

This edition is published with permission from Bloomsbury Publishing Plc.
50 Bedford Square, London WC1B3DP

Library of Congress Cataloging-in-Publication Data
A catalog record for this title is available from the Library of Congress

ISBN: 978-93-93715-12-8

Typeset in 10/13pt Utopia by Phoenix Photosetting, Chatham, Kent
Printed and bound in India by Replika Press Pvt. Ltd.

Contents

Preface vii

1 Introduction 1

2 Discourse 24

3 Design 45

4 Production 66

5 Distribution 86

6 Issues for the multimodal agenda 111

References 134

Index 139

Preface

This book, though modest in size, has had a longer history than we anticipated. When we started, we intended to write something like a complete 'guide to multimodal analysis'. But we soon realised that discussing the different modes (language, image, music, sound, gesture, and so on) separately was not good enough. Somehow we had to try to develop *multimodal concepts*, a framework that could apply across all these modes, the outline of a theory of the 'language of multimedia' (rather than of the 'languages' of gesture, music, and so on). This proved harder than we thought. Several early versions were torn up; several times we had to start over. Several times we even considered giving up. It was not until we began to incorporate the idea of *practice* more fully, until we moved from that idea of 'the language of multimedia' to the idea of 'communication', and from questions like 'what *is* a mode' to questions like 'how do people use the variety of semiotic resources to make signs in concrete social contexts', that we began to see some light at the end of the tunnel.

Even now, after almost seven years of discussing these issues, we do not feel we have been able to come to an agreement about them all. No doubt the attentive reader will spot the traces of these unfinished dialogues and unresolved issues in our text. But perhaps this is a good thing. After all, it was our intention to start a discussion, to open up the question of multimodality, not to close it.

We would like to thank our editor, Lesley Riddle, who patiently waited for the completion of this book, as well as the many people on whose ideas we have drawn, not least our colleagues and students at the Institute of Education, the London College of Printing and Cardiff University. And we would like to thank our partners, Jill and Laura, who must have wondered whether anything was ever going to come out of those weekly meetings in the cafés of London parks.

1 Introduction

Multimodality

For some time now, there has been, in Western culture, a distinct preference for monomodality. The most highly valued genres of writing (literary novels, academic treatises, official documents and reports, etc.) came entirely without illustration, and had graphically uniform, dense pages of print. Paintings nearly all used the same support (canvas) and the same medium (oils), whatever their style or subject. In concert performances all musicians dressed identically and only conductor and soloists were allowed a modicum of bodily expression. The specialised theoretical and critical disciplines which developed to speak of these arts became equally monomodal: one language to speak about language (linguistics), another to speak about art (art history), yet another to speak about music (musicology), and so on, each with its own methods, its own assumptions, its own technical vocabulary, its own strengths and its own blind spots.

More recently this dominance of monomodality has begun to reverse. Not only the mass media, the pages of magazines and comic strips for example, but also the documents produced by corporations, universities, government departments etc., have acquired colour illustrations and sophisticated layout and typography. And not only the cinema and the semiotically exuberant performances and videos of popular music, but also the avant-gardes of the 'high culture' arts have begun to use an increasing variety of materials and to cross the boundaries between the various art, design and performance disciplines, towards multimodal *Gesamtkunstwerke*, multimedia events, and so on.

The desire for crossing boundaries inspired twentieth-century semiotics. The main schools of semiotics all sought to develop a theoretical framework applicable to all semiotic modes, from folk costume to poetry, from traffic signs to classical music, from fashion to the theatre. Yet there was also a paradox. In our own work on visual semiotics (Kress and Van Leeuwen, 1996), we, too, were in a sense 'specialists' of the image, still standing with one foot in the world of monomodal disciplines. But at the same time we aimed at a common terminology for all semiotic modes, and stressed that, within a given social-cultural domain, the 'same' meanings can often be expressed in different semiotic modes.

In this book we make this move our primary aim; and so we explore the common principles behind multimodal communication. We move away from the idea that the different modes in multimodal texts have strictly bounded and framed specialist tasks, as in a film where images may provide the action, sync sounds a sense of realism, music a layer of emotion, and so on, with the editing process supplying the 'integration code', the means for synchronising the elements through a common rhythm (Van Leeuwen, 1985). Instead we move towards a view of multimodality in which common semiotic principles operate in and across different modes, and in which it is therefore quite possible for music to encode action, or images to encode emotion. This move comes, on our part, not because we think we had it all wrong before and have now suddenly seen the light. It is because we want to create a theory of semiotics appropriate to contemporary semiotic practice. In the past, and in many contexts still today, multimodal texts (such as films or newspapers) *were* organised as hierarchies of specialist modes integrated by an editing process. Moreover, they were produced in this way, with different, hierarchically organised specialists in charge of the different modes, and an editing process bringing their work together.

Today, however, in the age of digitisation, the different modes have technically become the same at some level of representation, and they can be operated by one multi-skilled person, using one interface, one mode of physical manipulation, so that he or she can ask, at every point: 'Shall I express this with sound or music?', 'Shall I say this visually or verbally?', and so on. Our approach takes its point of departure from this new development, and seeks to provide the element that has so far been missing from the equation: the semiotic rather than the technical element, the question of how this technical possibility can be made to work semiotically, of how we might have, not only a unified and unifying technology, but also a unified and unifying semiotics.

Let us give one specific example. In *Reading Images* (1996) we discussed 'framing' as specific to visual communication. By 'framing' we meant, in that context, the way elements of a visual composition may be disconnected, marked off from each other, for instance by framelines, pictorial framing devices (boundaries formed by the edge of a building, a tree, etc.), empty space between elements, discontinuities of colour, and so on. The concept also included the ways in which elements of a composition may be connected to each other, through the absence of disconnection devices, through vectors, and through continuities and similarities of colour, visual shape and so on. The significance is that disconnected elements will be read as, in some sense, separate and independent, perhaps even as contrasting units of meaning, whereas connected elements will be read as belonging together in some sense, as continuous or complementary. Arnheim's discussion of Titian's *Noli Me Tangere* (1982: 112) provides an example: '[Christ's] staff acts as a visual boundary between the figures', he comments, and 'Magdalen breaks the visual separation ... by the aggressive act of her right arm' (*see* Fig. 1.1).

Figure 1.1 *Noli Me Tangere*

But clearly framing is a multimodal principle. There can be framing, not only between the elements of a visual composition, but also between the bits of writing in a newspaper or magazine layout (Kress and Van Leeuwen, 1998), between the people in an office, the seats in a train or restaurant (e.g. private compartments versus sharing tables), the dwellings in a suburb, etc., and such instances of framing will also be realised by 'framelines', empty space, discontinuities of all kinds, and so on. In time-based modes, moreover, 'framing' becomes 'phrasing' and is realised by the short pauses and discontinuities of various kinds (rhythmic, dynamic, etc.) which separate the phrases of speech, of music and of actors' movements. We have here a common semiotic principle, though differently realised in different semiotic modes.

The search for such common principles can be undertaken in different ways. It is possible to work out detailed grammars for each and every semiotic mode, detailed accounts of what can be 'said' with that mode and how, using for each of the grammars as much as possible (as much as the materiality of the mode makes that plausible) the same approach and the same terminology. At the end of this process it would then become possible to overlay these different grammars and to see where they overlap and where they do not, which areas are common to which of the modes, and in which respects the modes are specialised. There have by now been a number of attempts at devising such grammars, all based to a greater or lesser degree on the semiotic theories of Halliday (Halliday 1978, 1985) and Hodge and Kress (1988), and hence sharing a common approach – for instance the semiotics of action of Martinec (1996, 1998), the semiotics of images of O'Toole (1994) and Kress and Van Leeuwen (1996), the semiotics of sound of Van Leeuwen (1999), the semiotics of theatre of Martin (1997) and McInnes (1998), and so on.

We are and will continue to be part of this enterprise ourselves. But in this book we want to pause, as it were, to take stock of what general picture is emerging. We want to sketch a multimodal theory of communication based, not on ideas which naturalise the characteristics of semiotic modes by equating sensory channels and semiotic modes, but on an analysis of the specificities and common traits of semiotic modes which takes account of their social, cultural and historical production, of when and how the modes of production are specialised or multi-skilled, hierarchical or team-based, of when and how technologies are specialised or multi-purpose, and so on.

The issue of meaning in a multimodal theory of communication

We indicated in the preface that it was our focus on *practices* and our use of the notion of *resources*, rather than a focus on fixed, stable entities, which allowed us to make progress with a multimodal approach to representation and communciation. In relation to one specific question this has been particularly crucial, namely the question of meaning. The traditional linguistic account is one in which *meaning is made once*, so to speak. By contrast, we see the multimodal resources which are available in a culture used to make meanings in any and every sign, at every level, and in any mode. Where traditional linguistics had defined language as a system that worked through *double articulation*, where a message was an articulation as a form and as a meaning, we see multimodal texts as making meaning in multiple articulations. Here we sketch the four domains of practice in which meanings are dominantly made. We call these *strata* to show a relation to Hallidayan functional linguistics, for reasons of the potential compatibility of description of different modes. We do not however see strata as being hierarchically ordered, as *one above the other* for instance, or some such interpretation. Our four strata are discourse, design, production and distribution.

Discourse

Discourses are socially constructed knowledges of (some aspect of) reality. By 'socially constructed' we mean that they have been developed in specific social contexts, and in ways which are appropriate to the interests of social actors in these contexts, whether these are very broad contexts ('Western Europe') or not (a particular family), explicitly institutionalised contexts (newspapers) or not (dinner-table conversations), and so on. For instance, the 'ethnic conflict' discourse of war can be drawn on by Western journalists when reporting civil wars in Africa or former Yugoslavia, but it is also an available resource in certain kinds of conversation, in airport thrillers or in movies set in Africa, and so on. War discourses involve both a certain version of what actually happens in wars, of who is involved, what they do, and where and when, and a set of interpretations, evaluative judgements, critical or justifying arguments and so on, related to wars or aspects of them. The 'ethnic conflict' discourses of war in newspapers, for instance, serve the interests of the countries in which the newspapers are produced, as perceived by the projected readership of the papers. Hence they usually leave out mention of the influence of colonisation and de-colonisation and defend non-intervention by constructing conflicts as going back hundreds of years or more, to mention just two aspects. There are other discourses of war, for instance discourses in which 'economics' or 'ideology' feature as explanatory categories. These will include and exclude other participants and events, link their versions of what actually goes on in wars with other interpretations, judgements, arguments etc., and serve other interests. And while some discourses include a great deal of emphasis on the actual events and provide few interpretations or arguments, others form a storehouse of abstract interpretation and argument but make do with only a broad and general version of what warring parties actually do.

Any discourse may be realised in different ways. The 'ethnic conflict' discourse of war, for instance, may be realised as (part of) a dinner-table conversation, a television documentary, a newspaper feature, an airport thriller, and so on. In other words, discourse is relatively independent of genre, of mode and (somewhat less) of design. Yet discourses can only be realised in semiotic modes which have developed the means for realising them. In the 1920s, following the Russian Revolution, film had not developed the means for realising Marxist discourses. Hence a film-maker like Eisenstein, for instance, who dreamt of filming Marx's *Capital,* set about developing his method of 'dialectical montage' (Eisenstein, 1949), and in the process extended the semiotic reach of the medium.

Design

Design stands midway between content and expression. It is the conceptual side of expression, and the expression side of conception. Designs are (uses of) semiotic resources, in all semiotic modes and combinations of semiotic modes. Designs are means to realise discourses in the context of a given communication situation. But designs also add something new: they realise the communication situation which changes socially constructed knowledge into social (inter-) action. Consider writers who write thrillers in a setting of 'ethnic conflict', for instance: at the same time as they realise the 'ethnic conflict' discourse of war, they realise a particular mode of interaction in which it is their purpose to entertain an audience of a particular kind. In doing so, designs may either follow well-trodden paths of habit, convention, tradition, or prescription, or be innovative and ground-breaking, just as discourses may either express common sense, or be innovative and perhaps even subversive.

But design is still separate from the actual material production of the semiotic product or the actual material articulation of the semiotic event. The resources on which design draws, the semiotic modes, are still abstract, capable of being realised in different materialities. Language, for instance, is a semiotic mode because it can be realised either as speech or as writing, and writing is a semiotic mode too, because it can be realised as engraving in stone, as calligraphy on certificates, as print on glossy paper, and all these media add a further layer of signification. The writer of the 'ethnic conflict' thriller, apart from using language, also uses the resources of the mode of narrative in designing the thriller. And this mode is separate from the *medium* of the printed book in which it will be produced. The same design may be realised in different media. The same story may become a mainstream movie or an airport thriller, given a shared communicative purpose and conception of who the audience is. Quite different skills are of course required for actually writing the book or producing the movie.

This view of design also applies to semiotic practices which do not so clearly have a 'subject matter'. An architect, for instance, designs (but does not build) a house or a block of apartments. The discourse provides a certain view of how houses are lived in, of how many and which kinds of people live in houses, of what they do in their houses, coupled with interpretations of why they live the way they do, and arguments which critique or defend these ways of life. The design of the house then conceptualises how to give shape to this discourse in the form of a house or a type of apartment. According to architect Chris Timmerman (1998: 11–12), there are architectural projects 'which are never built, but remain on paper, in the mind, on the hard disk', and they often are ground-breaking architecture because 'one can allow oneself the luxury and freedom of concentrating on the spatial experiential aspects of architecture as opposed to the economic and structural reality of building'. He quotes Virilio (1997: 26) to support the idea that architecture can be realised in several different materialities, not only in the form of buildings, but also, for instance, as interactive computer programmes: 'While the topical City was once constructed around the *gate* and the *port*, the teletopical metacity is now reconstructed around the window and the teleport, that is to say, around the screen and the time slot'.

Production

'Production' refers to the organisation of the expression, to the actual material articulation of the semiotic event or the actual material production of the semiotic artefact. A whole other set of skills is involved here: technical skills, skills of the hand and the eye, skills related not to semiotic modes, but to semiotic *media*. We use the term 'medium' here in the sense of 'medium of execution' (the material substance drawn into culture and worked over cultural time), the sense in which artists use it when they speak of the medium of 'oil', or 'tempera on paper', or 'bronze mounted on marble base'; it applies of course also to media which do not produce traces that last beyond the moment of articulation, such as speech or music.

Sometimes design and production, mode and medium, are hard to separate. Improvising musicians, for instance, both design and perform their music. They rehearse, perhaps, but even in rehearsals it may be difficult to know where 'design' ends and 'performance' begins. In other contexts there is a gap between the two, and they separate out in different roles: composers design the music and performers execute it. In that case the work of performers will often be seen as adding little meaning, as 'merely' realising and making audible the intentions of the composer as faithfully as possible, and as adding, at best, the 'expressiveness' which black dots on paper do not have. Linguists have the same view of language: the expression plane does not add meaning and 'merely' realises what can also be written down, without loss of essential meaning. Teachers, for instance, may either design their own lessons or merely 'execute' a detailed syllabus designed by expert educators. In other words, when design and production separate, design becomes a means for controlling the actions of others, the potential for a unity between discourse, design and production diminishes, and there is no longer room for the 'producers' to make the design 'their own', to add their own accent. In all this, writing and its ability to provide detailed 'scripts' and 'prescriptions' ('pro-grammes') for action has undoubtedly played a pivotal role.

Distribution

As already mentioned, the stratum of expression needs to be stratified further. Musical performers may need the technicians who record the music on tape and disc for preservation and distribution; designers of a product may need the crafts people who produce the prototype of the product, and the other crafts people who produce the mould for mass production.

Distribution, too, tends to be seen as not semiotic, as not adding any meaning, as merely facilitating the pragmatic functions of preservation and distribution. Just as it is the performer's job to be faithful to the intentions of the composer, so it is the recording and sound-mixing engineers' job to achieve 'high fidelity': 'I want to make records which will sound in the public's home exactly like what they would hear in the best seat in an acoustically perfect hall', said EMI producer Walter Legge (quoted in Chanan, 1995: 133). But the public's home is not a concert hall, and acoustically perfect halls do not exist. Introducing orchestral music into the home and being able to hear the same performance over and over already fundamentally changes the meaning of music, for example through the loss of 'aura' of which Walter Benjamin wrote (1977). As time moves on, distribution media may, in part or in whole, turn into production media. The contribution of the sound engineer may become equal to that of the musician, with parameters like reverb used, not to (re)create 'the acoustically perfect hall', but to act as independent signifiers, able, for instance, to make sounds either 'interior' and subjective or 'exterior' and objective, as in many contemporary dance music mixes (Van Leeuwen, 1999), where the drum and bass are so 'close up' that they do not seem to be played in an actual space at all, but inside the head or body, in a space where all sound is absorbed instantly.

Articulation and interpretation

The terms we have used ('design', 'production', 'distribution') might suggest that we are looking at multimodal communication only from the point of view of the producers. But this is not so. Our model applies equally to interpretation. Indeed, we define communication as only having taken place when there has been both articulation and interpretation. (In fact we might go one step further and say that communication depends on some 'interpretive community' having decided that some aspect of the world has been articulated in order to be interpreted.) Interpreters need to supply semiotic knowledge at all four of the levels we have distinguished. At the level of distribution, they need to know, for instance, whether they are dealing with a reproduction or an original, even in cases where the boundaries are deliberately blurred, as in some of Andy Warhol's work. They also need to understand the respective values of 'design' and 'production'. Adorno (1976, 1978), for whom 'structural listening' was the highest form of music listening, condemned jazz because of the simplicity of what we call here its 'design' (the simple chord schemas of Broadway songs). For this he was taken to task by Middleton (1990), who argued that he did not know how to appreciate the semiotic richness of what we call here the 'production' of jazz singers and musicians. The same phenomenon sometimes occurs in comparisons between literary novels and their movie adaptations.

Design and discourse play their role in interpretation too, even though a given interaction may be experienced differently, and a given discourse interpreted differently, from the way it was intended. A story may be written to entertain, but an interpreter may not be entertained because of the story's built-in ethnocentric bias against the interpreter's ethnic group. A product may be designed to make its use easy, but certain users may not appreciate products which do their thinking for them. Such users operate from a different discourse, a different conception of what is involved in that task and a different set of associated values and ideas. Which discourses interpreters or users may bring to bear on a semiotic product or event has everything to do, in turn, with their place in the social and cultural world, and also with the content. The degree to which intention and interpretation will match depends on context. For instance, most of us interpret a traffic sign the same way (there are differences: do you slow down when amber appears, or do you speed up?), unless it is particularly badly designed, or unless an interpreter has recently emerged from a place where there is no traffic. But when, for instance, a traffic sign is displayed as an *objet trouvé* in an art gallery, our interpretations are likely to differ significantly.

Stratal configurations

At the level of the social organisation of semiotic production different configurations of discourse, design, production and distribution may occur. Three of these may be merged for instance, as in everyday conversational speech, where any speaker or listener incorporates discourse, design and production skills and probably experiences them subjectively as one and the same. Nevertheless, even here they do remain distinct strata. Speakers need access to discourses, knowledges which are socially structured for the purpose at hand; they need to know how to formulate these knowledges in the appropriate register and how to embed them in an (inter)active event; and they need to be able to speak. Much as we might take these skills for granted and see them as a unified whole, they are distinct, as would quickly become apparent if any one of them became impaired.

At the other end of the scale from everyday conversation we might have the speech, say, of professional voice-over specialists. Here the division of labour is maximised. Each stratum involves different people and different skills. Expert sources provide the discourse, scriptwriters the design, voice specialists the voices, recording engineers the recordings, and so on. Yet the division of labour is not total. The experts will be handpicked for their understanding of what the media need and their ability to provide the kinds of discourse appropriate to television documentaries. The scriptwriters will have to know something about television production so as not to write things which cannot be filmed or are too expensive to film, and so as to make good use of the medium's specific 'production values'. The voice-over specialists must understand what they are reading and take account of the requirements of the recording engineers, by keeping their voice at an even level, not rustling the paper, and so on. In other words, what we shall call 'stratal uncoupling' is never absolute.

Moreover, the two types of semiotic production exist in the same society. We live in a world where discourse, design and production no longer form a unity, where teachers are trained to teach without any reference to what they might be teaching, managers to manage without any reference to what they might be managing, interviewees to being interviewed without any reference to what the interviews might be about. Again, in many contexts we are encouraged or even obliged to reproduce discourses 'in our own words', that is, without also reproducing their design. And we know that design and production are sometimes coupled, so that different productions of the same design can be regarded as 'saying the same thing' (e.g. performances of classical music) and sometimes uncoupled (e.g. jazz performances, where two different versions of the same tune might be 'saying' something quite different). This makes our semiotic landscape fundamentally different from that of oral societies where knowledge is indissolubly welded to its formulation, and where the distinction between 'what you say' and 'how you say it' would be difficult to understand.

It is above all the invention of writing which has made this possible, which has disrupted the direct link between discourse and production that can still be observed for instance in the semiotic production of young children (Kress, 1997). Writing has produced 'language', a semiotic resource no longer tied to its material realisation, no longer just 'tongue' (the original meaning of the word 'language') or 'inscription' (the word 'graphic' originally meant 'make marks', 'scratch'), but 'syntax' (a word which originated as a military term, meaning 'organisation', 'battle formation', and only later came also to mean 'organise', 'write', 'compose'). As such, writing can be used to create order, and to govern human action, and make it predictable, repeatable, whether this is internalised as a set of grammatical rules, or externalised as a script, a written procedure, a programme, a syllabus, etc. It is only in certain marginal or marginalised fields, or during times when new discourses, new designs, and/or new modes of production and distribution are needed, that a more immediate link between discourse and production is maintained or reinstated, and that other less prescriptive and systematic semiotic principles come to the fore.

In this book we will discuss two such principles in particular. The first is *provenance*, 'where signs come from'. The idea here is that we constantly 'import' signs from other contexts (another era, social group, culture) into the context in which we are now making a new sign, in order to signify ideas and values which are associated with that other context by those who import the sign. To take a musical example, in the 1960s the Beatles introduced the sound of the sitar into their music to signify values which, in the 'psychedelic' youth culture of that time, were associated with the sitar's country of origin: meditation, drugs as expansion of consciousness, and so on. The idea of 'provenance' is closely related to the ideas of 'myth' and 'connotation' as introduced into semiotics by Roland Barthes (1972, 1977).

The second is *experiential meaning potential*, the idea that signifiers have a meaning potential deriving from what it is we *do* when we produce them, and from our ability to turn action into knowledge, to extend our practical experience metaphorically, and to grasp similar extensions made by others. To give an example, the sound quality of 'breathiness' derives its meaning from our knowledge of the kinds of situation in which it may occur – when we are out of breath, for instance, and when we are unable to control our breathing due to excitement. Hence 'breathiness' can become a signifier for intimacy and sensuality, for instance in singing styles or in the speech in television commercials for products that can be associated with intimacy or sensuality. The same principle may once upon a time have helped create the words we now use: think of the way the words 'language' and 'tongue' both require a maximum amount of tongue movement from the front to the back of the mouth. The idea of 'experiential meaning potential' is close to the view of 'metaphor' elaborated in Lakoff and Johnson (1980).

Thus the social stratification of semiotic production is mirrored by the stratification of the semiotic resources themselves. And while it can be argued that 'distribution', at this stage, has not yet been internalised as a 'stratum' of semiotic modes, it is at least possible that new technologies, increasingly ubiquitous, multi-purpose and 'natural' in terms of their interfaces, will help create a fourth dimension of communication in the same way that writing created a third – and this time not at the cost of a decrease in multimodality.

Stephanie's bedroom as a multimodal text

We will use the discourse, design and production of children's bedrooms, and of texts about children's bedrooms, as a first example of our approach. 'Children's bedroom discourses' form part of 'family life' discourses, socially constructed knowledges about who forms part of families, what family members do (together or separately), where they do it, which outsiders may take part in which family activities, and so on. There are always likely to be several such discourses, associated, for instance, with different social classes or ethnic groups (in Britain and Australia many middle-class families set a specific space aside for 'entertaining', for instance), or based on deviant practices, wrong ways of living in a family home which therefore form a danger for other families (such as the demonic children's bedroom of the next door kid Sid in Disney's *Toy Story*).

Discourses which are still in the process of being elaborated and have not yet become common sense and subject to what Bourdieu has called 'genesis amnesia' are of particular interest. Early socialist 'family life' discourses are an example of this. They were developed in the early decades of the twentieth century in several European cities. The Amsterdam councillor Wibaut, for instance, began to visit working-class families at home and found 'many dwellings where large families with six, seven, eight children lived, cooked, worked and slept in one room' (Roegholt, 1976: 13). In 1904 he inaugurated a policy of declaring such dwellings uninhabitable and building new suburbs for their occupants. In the process he and others developed a discourse of workers' family lives, in which workers would see their homes as fortresses for protecting their families against a threatening outside world, and as a place to relax after a hard day's work. Architects then realised this discourse in buildings which indeed looked like fortresses (*see* Fig. 1.2). There were forbidding façades, heavy doors with small barred windows, hidden in deep and monumental

Figure 1.2 *Amsterdam workers' housing complex built 1917–21, architect Michel de Klerk*

entrance recesses, and windows so high that the occupants needed to stand on a stool to look through them – protection against the threatening outside world and promotion of inward-looking family values was the motivation (Roegholt, 1976: 32). Hygiene was another key theme, at least for the city planners, because the workers themselves often longed for their remembered cosy alcoves, used the toilets as storage and the showers as broom cupboards, and did not appreciate the washing and drying spaces in the attics which had been intended to free them from the smell of drying washing: 'The women did not like to do their washing communally and preferred to keep their underwear to themselves' (Roegholt, 1976: 41).

Public housing projects in Vienna were based on a similar discourse. Eventually some of it became enshrined in the law, which stipulates that there has to be 'approximately 10 square metres for every person', 'a kitchen and suitable sanitary facilities for every household' and 'a bedroom separate from the living-room in the case of families with children'. Today this law is used to prevent immigrant workers from being reunited with their families, and some magistrates further elaborate on it in an attempt to prove that the 'family life' discourse of the immigrant workers is not *ortsüblich*, not 'in accordance with local tradition' (Van Leeuwen and Wodak, 1999). One magistrate, for instance, rejected an application because the applicant's apartment did not have 'space for the social and cultural development of the family'. The apartment of another lacked a separate bedroom for the daughter, a situation which the magistrate judged not to be 'beneficial for the educational development of the child'. The applicants themselves had a different view of family life which did not include closed doors, and protested that 'close spatial proximity between parents and children is important'.

The pictures of children's bedrooms in *House Beautiful* type magazines rarely show school-age children or teenagers. Only three- or four-year-olds are depicted, or mentioned by name in the text. An article about three-year-old Stephanie's room (*House Beautiful*, September 1996: 160–2) contains some details of what young children actually do in their room: 'The multicoloured sofa provides Stephanie with somewhere to sit and read her books'; 'Handy pegs were attached to the bright yellow dado that runs round the room to make it easy for Stephanie to hang up her coats and toys'. Stephanie also has a miniature theatre in her room. 'I sing and dance with my friends up here', she says, 'We dress up and act in our own plays – it's great fun.' She features in two of the pictures, once looking up from a picture book, once holding up a marionette on the stage of her miniature theatre (Fig. 1.3). Other pictures provide evidence of at least two other activities, drawing (a blackboard on the door of the wardrobe) and sleeping (a bed with a colourful patchwork quilt).

Three-year-old Noel is shown in his room holding a toy car (*House Beautiful*, September 1996: 32): 'Most of the time you will find him playing with his model cars'. And three-year-old Will is shown in two pictures, building a railway track in one, and playing with a multi-level garage in another. A corner of a bed and a chest

Figure 1.3 *Stephanie in her room (*House Beautiful, *September 1996: 162)*

of drawers suggest other activities (*Ideal Homes and Lifestyle*, September 1998: 100).

As a social construction of what kind of (three-year-old) children live in 'beautiful homes' and of what these children do in their bedrooms (playing with toys; neatly putting toys and clothes away; sleeping, always by themselves), these discourses are clearly selective. They are also gendered: although there are toys in her room, Stephanie does not play with toys, but reads, sings, dances and dresses up. Noel and Will play with trains and toys. The magazines also contain pictures of the rooms of some older children. These usually include a desk, typically with a desk light and a globe: a place for home-work. The computer interface in Figure 1.4 shows the children's bedroom as a virtual space for play as well as work, with toys stacked on shelves on the left and labelled drawers for 'work' on the right.

A totally different family-life discourse emerges from the pictures in the 1998/99 IKEA catalogue. As the occasional writings on blackboards, book spines etc. indicate, the pictures were all taken in Sweden. Here children often play together (a boy and a girl are reading together, for instance), and they also play with their parents (a father is served a make-believe cup of tea in his daughter's room). Teenagers have computers and hi-fis in rooms with pictures of pop stars and sports heroes on the walls: 'After a certain age, children want their own bit of personal space, somewhere to keep them happy, and keep all their stuff, somewhere to tell all their friends about' (p. 67).

Discourses not only provide versions of who does what, when and where, they add evaluations, interpretations and arguments to these versions. We have already discussed some of the arguments of the socialist family-life discourses of the early decades of this century. In magazines of the *House Beautiful* type, the arguments are presented as common sense and are not explicitly formulated. Motivations come across most often through certain aspects of the rooms themselves, for instance the colour scheme, and through value-laden adjectives. Let us have another look at Stephanie's room. There is a strong emphasis on colour, both in the text and in the pictures, and the colours are called, on the one hand, 'bright', 'bold', 'dramatic' etc., and on the other hand 'sunny' and 'cheerful'. The article as a whole ends as follows: 'With so much inspiration in her new room, Stephanie is full of ideas about what she wants to be when she grows up. She's clearly had plenty of practice at being a mountain climber [this refers to fixtures in the room which were too high for her before the redecoration], and now she can add acting and interior design to her CV!'

This children's bedroom is clearly a pedagogic tool, a medium for communicating to the child, in the language of interior design, the qualities (already complex: 'bold', yet also 'sunny' and 'cheerful'), the pleasures ('singing and dancing with your friends'), the duties (orderly management of possessions and, eventually, 'work'), and the kind of future her parents desire for her. This destiny, moreover, is communicated to her in a language that is to be *lived*, lived as an individual identity-building and identity-confirming experience in that individual bedroom. Such a pedagogic

Figure 1.4 *Packard Bell 'Kidspace' interface*

discourse is only one of a number of possible 'children's bedroom' discourses. There are and will be others. But they have not found their way into the British magazines we have looked at.

The pedagogic 'children's bedroom' discourse can be realised in a number of ways. It can be realised as an actual children's room, through the multimodal 'language of interior design' in which meanings are realised by spatial arrangements (the 'dado' which runs right around the room and makes 'putting your things away' literally an omnipresent feature of the room); by choice of furniture (the sofa, a place for reading); by colour schemes (the 'bold' and yet also 'sunny' and 'cheerful' colours); and so on. All this has to be conceptualised as 'design' before it can be produced, regardless of whether the parents themselves both design and produce the redecoration, use a professional designer, or follow an explicit pre-existing model designed or endorsed by an expert.

The same discourse can be realised as a *House Beautiful* article, in the text and pictures of children's books, or in IKEA catalogues. Here the practice of communicating pedagogic messages through the design of a children's bedroom is represented in other contexts, contexts such as the magazine, or the children's book. And these contexts have their own communicative purposes and their own 'recipients'. The children's book *Mark and Mandy* (Leete-Hodge, n.d.), for instance, is written to be read to young children and deals with the transition from home to school. The two children are apprehensive about 'the first day', but in the end school turns out to be enjoyable, and the first day at school the most memorable event of their lives. The children's rooms are implicated: somewhere along the way Mandy's room acquires a new piece of furniture, 'a fine blackboard and easel, with a packet of white chalks and a yellow duster, just like school'. Like Stephanie's room, *Mark and Mandy* has a pedagogic purpose, 'getting children prepared for school'. But it uses a different method, the method of storytelling. *House Beautiful* seeks to provide models for creating the right kind of setting for the right kind of family life. The houses it features in the articles are 'ideal homes', 'dream houses' to aspire to – the homes of celebrities and of model couples who have tastefully renovated their 'rustic-style cottages' and 'spacious Georgian houses'. The houses featured in the advertisements, on the other hand, are a little more downmarket.

The skills required for designing *House Beautiful* features about children's bedrooms differ from those required for designing children's bedrooms. They include the skill of writing in a style appropriate for the purpose at hand, of producing the right kind of photographs, designing the right kind of layout, and so on. For one thing, the audiences for the two differ: parents as readers in one case, children as users in the other. The pictures, for instance, must be 'analytical', pictures which clearly show how the room is made up of its component parts (Kress and Van Leeuwen, 1996). The language similarly must foreground place, furniture, room fixtures, and show how the room and its various parts 'hang together'. But language does this in a different way from that of image, for instance by 'thematising' the elements of the room (Halliday, 1985), putting them at the head of the sentences:

> Handy pegs were attached to the bright yellow dado that runs around the room to make it easy for Stephanie to hang up her coats and toys.

Writers of children's books would design the same content yet again differently. They would most probably 'thematise' character and action, add some detail about the action perhaps, and reduce the detail of the description of the room and its fixtures and furniture:

> Stephanie neatly hung her coats and toys on the yellow dado in her room.

Children's illustrated books would in their turn be different. Whereas most of the pictures in *House Beautiful* do not show people, most of the pictures in children's books do, again to put the emphasis on characters and actions, the two vital elements in any story.

Design also involves a knowledge of the relationship between words and pictures. The *House Beautiful* article features no less than ten pictures on three pages, and they occupy by far the greatest amount of space on every one of these pages. After all, pictures are much better at conveying how furniture is arranged in a room, and at 'describing' exactly what a sofa or a colour looks like. In spatial matters, language comes a poor second to image. But then, language is used for other things: to tell the story of the way the house was acquired and the room decorated, to link the layout of the room to the child's activities, to reinforce the meanings of the colour scheme by means of evaluative adjectives, and to bring out, however implicitly, the pedagogic 'message' of the room. The 'redecoration' story starts the article, and the 'pedagogic message' ends it. In other words, the two semiotic modes are given complementary specialist tasks, just like the photographer and the writer.

The design of the article is quite similar to other features in *House Beautiful*, and to features in other, similar magazines. Such relative standardisation is typical of much journalistic work, and derives to quite some extent from the standardised routines of journalistic work and the intricate division of labour of magazine production. Yet, there is no 'recipe'. There is tradition, but not prescription, a formula, but not a template, and it is this that makes it possible for the journalists, the photographers and the layout artists to feel that every job presents a new challenge, a new problem to be solved (Bell and Van Leeuwen, 1994: 174). Although semiotic modes have developed in this field, as can be demonstrated by linguistic analysis of the 'generic structure' of journalistic writing and television interviews (e.g. Van Leeuwen, 1987; Bell, 1991; Iedema, 1993; Bell and Van Leeuwen, 1994), the writers, photographers and designers can 'make these styles their own' and develop their own 'accents'. It is not quite the textual equivalent of wearing a uniform, but rather the textual equivalent of wearing a business suit, a prescribed form of dress which nevertheless leaves the wearer some room for a personal touch.

House Beautiful presents the story of how Stephanie's room was produced as a new invention, rather than as the parents' choice from a mental or actual catalogue of socially available possibilities. Like the socialist city fathers of early twentieth-century Amsterdam and Vienna, Stephanie's parents knew that rooms have to be 'light' and 'airy', but unfortunately Stephanie's room did not get much light. How could they resolve this?

> They didn't know where to begin until a friend came round with a patchwork duvet cover he'd bought as a present for Stephanie. Boasting all the colours of the rainbow, it was perfect for a youngster's bedroom and provided plenty of inspiration for a new look.

This duvet cover is shown in one of the photos. It is made up of a number of squares featuring simple, basic pictures of objects (a boat, a teapot, a car), in bright primary colours. They are instances of a recognisable genre of contemporary pictures and toys for very young children: 'essential' locomotives, cars, planes, birds, trees, in Mondrian-like colours. Yet this conventional colour scheme is here presented as a unique solution to the problem of how to make an existing space, which was not really designed for that purpose, fit a discourse. It is a problem which many families face when selecting an apartment or house which was perhaps built in a different era for a different kind of family life: how to accommodate it to contemporary family life. Why is this? Is it because families should be seen to have a unique identity, and not one that is, as it were, pre-designed, 'pre-fabricated' by dominant 'designs'? Or is it to justify the magazine's presentation of this room as a 'model' room, an original creation, a piece of art, well worth imitating by lesser parents?

Finally, whereas *House Beautiful* and *Mark and Mandy* are mass-produced and distributed to a dispersed readership, Stephanie's bedroom is of course unique: there is only one and it can only be found in the town where Stephanie lives. There is no 'distribution' stratum in the case of architecture or interior design. However, new technology may yet change this. Virtual reality can now reproduce a given space in such a way that one can walk through it and have a multi-sensory experience of it. At present, not least as a result of the encumbrances of goggles, datagloves etc., the difference between actual and virtual spaces seems overwhelming. Virtual reality entails a complete loss of actual physical presence. But so did to Walter Benjamin the difference between the work of art and its mechanical reproduction: a complete loss of 'aura'. How many of us still feel an essential lack when looking at the reproduction of a work of art, or listening to the recording of a musical performance? The time may yet come when little girls can while away countless hours in virtual rooms, and experience a variety of identities, duties and pleasures realised in a *spatial* mass medium, a globally distributable language of interior design.

Conclusion

In this chapter we have sketched the outline of a theory of multimodal communication. We have defined multimodality as the use of several semiotic modes in the design of a semiotic product or event, together with the particular way in which these modes are combined – they may for instance reinforce each other ('say the same thing in different ways'), fulfil complementary roles, as in the *House Beautiful* article about Stephanie's bedroom, or be hierarchically ordered, as in action films, where action is dominant, with music adding a touch of emotive colour and sync sound a touch of realistic 'presence'. We defined communication as a process in which a semiotic product or event is both articulated or produced *and* interpreted or used. It follows from this definition that we consider the production and use of designed objects and environments as a form of communication: we used the example of a room, but could also have used a designed object as our example.

The main concepts we have introduced in the chapter are recapitulated in the discussion of terms below.

Recapitulation

Strata: The basis of stratification is the distinction between the *content* and the *expression* of communication, which includes that between the signifieds and the signifiers of the signs used. As a result of the invention of writing, the content stratum could be further stratified into **discourse** and **design**. As a result of the invention of modern communication technologies, the expression stratum could be further stratified into **production** and **distribution**.

The stratification of semiotic resources has its counterpart in the social stratification of semiotic production, certainly in the early stages of the use of new communication technologies. In later stages it may become possible for one person to produce the product or event from start to finish, as is beginning to happen today with interactive multimedia.

In this book we argue that production and distribution produce their own layers of signification. Indeed, we have argued that semiotic modes and design ideas usually flow out of production, using principles of semiosis typical for production, such as **provenance** and **experiential meaning potential**.

Discourse: Discourses are socially situated forms of knowledge about (aspects of) reality. This includes knowledge of the events constituting that reality (who is involved, what takes place, where and when it takes place, and so on) as well as a set of related evaluations, purposes, interpretations and legitimations.

People often have several alternative discourses available with respect to a particular aspect of reality. They will then use the one that is most appropriate to the interests of the communication situation in which they find themselves.

Design: Designs are conceptualisations of the form of semiotic products and events. Three things are designed simultaneously: (1) a formulation of a discourse or combination of discourses, (2) a particular (inter)action, in which the discourse is embedded, and (3) a particular way of combining semiotic **modes**.

Design is separate from the actual material production of the semiotic product or event, and uses (abstract) semiotic modes as its resources. It may involve intermediate productions (musical scores, play scripts, blueprints, etc.) but the form these take is not the form in which the design is eventually to reach the public, and they tend be produced in as abstract a modality as possible, using austere methods of realisation that do not involve any form of realistic detail, texture, colour and so on.

Production: Production is the articulation in material form of semiotic products or events, whether in the form of a prototype that is still to be 'transcoded' into another form for purposes of distribution (e.g. a 35 mm telemovie) or in its final form (e.g. a videotape packaged for commercial distribution).

Production not only gives perceivable form to designs but adds meanings which flow directly from the physical process of articulation and the physical qualities of the materials used, for instance from the articulatory gestures involved in speech production, or from the weight, colour and texture of the material used by a sculptor.

Distribution: Distribution refers to the technical 're-coding' of semiotic products and events, for purposes of recording (e.g. tape recording, digital recording) and/or distribution (e.g. radio and television transmission, telephony).

Distribution technologies are generally not intended as production technologies, but as *re*-production technologies, and are therefore not meant to produce meaning themselves. However, they soon begin to acquire a semiotic potential of their own, and even unwanted 'noise' sources such as the scratches and discolorations of old film prints may become signifiers in their own right. In the age of digital media, however, the functions of production and distribution become technically integrated to a much greater extent.

Another key distinction in this chapter is the distinction between *mode*, which is on the 'content' side, and *medium*, which is on the 'expression' side.

Mode: Modes are semiotic resources which allow the simultaneous realisation of discourses and types of (inter)action. Designs then use these resources, combining semiotic modes, and selecting from the options which they make available according to the interests of a particular communication situation.

Modes can be realised in more than one production **medium**. Narrative is a mode because it allows discourses to be formulated in particular ways (ways which 'personify' and 'dramatise' discourses, among other things), because it constitutes a particular kind of interaction, and because it can be realised in a range of different media.

It follows that media become modes once their principles of semiosis begin to be conceived of in more abstract ways (as 'grammars' of some kind). This in turn will make it possible to realise them in a range of media. They lose their tie to a specific form of material realisation.

Medium: Media are the material resources used in the production of semiotic products and events, including both the tools and the materials used (e.g. the musical instrument and air; the chisel and the block of wood). They usually are specially produced for this purpose, not only in culture (ink, paint, cameras, computers), but also in nature (our vocal apparatus).

Recording and distribution media have been developed specifically for the recording and/or distribution of semiotic products and events which have already been materially realised by production media, and as such are not supposed to function semiotically. But in the course of their development, they usually start functioning as production media – just as production media may become design modes.

Lastly, we discussed the specific ways in which meaning is produced 'in production'. This is not always a matter of 'realising designs', in the way that a speech may realise what the speaker has prepared, or a building what the architect has designed, and it certainly does not usually happen in the 'arbitrary' ways which have been foregrounded by linguists. In fact, signification starts on the side of production, using semiotic principles which have not yet sedimented into conventions, traditions, grammars, or laws of design. Only eventually, as the particular medium gains in social importance, will more abstract modes of regulation ('grammars') develop, and the medium will become a mode. The opposite, modes becoming media again, is also possible. The science of physiognomy, for instance, lost its status as a result of its racist excesses, and now semiotic practices like casting are 'media' again, operating on the basis of primary semiotic principles such as 'provenance' and 'experiential meaning potential'.

Experiential meaning potential: This refers to the idea that material signifiers have a meaning potential that derives from what it is we *do* when we articulate them, and from our ability to extend our practical experience metaphorically and turn action into knowledge. This happens, for instance, with the textural characteristics of sound qualities (as when singers adopt a soft, breathy voice to signify sensuality), in the absence of a conventionalised 'system' of sound qualities (such as the symphony orchestra).

Provenance: This refers to the idea that signs may be 'imported' from one context (another era, social group, culture) into another, in order to signify the ideas and values associated with that other context by those who do the importing. This happens, for instance, in giving names to people, places or things (e.g. in naming a perfume 'Paris') when there is no 'code', no sedimented set of rules for naming perfumes.

2 Discourse

Discourse, mode, materiality

In our definition of discourse ('discourses are socially constructed knowledges of (some aspect of) reality') we have not, so far, moved explicitly away from two assumptions which underpin much of the work in discourse analysis carried out over the last two decades or so. These are, on the one hand, that discourse 'relates to language', or, perhaps more strongly, that discourse exists in language; and, on the other hand, perhaps paradoxically, that discourses 'just exist', irrespective of (any) material realisations. Both assumptions are often held simultaneously, so that what is talked about is the shape of discursive organisation, the characteristics of specific discourses; but this is talked about in terms of the appearance of discourses in the realisational mode of language. In our approach we want to adopt both positions: the notion that discourses have an existence which is (somehow) separate from their mode of realisation, and, of course, the idea that discourses appear in the mode of language, among many others. By contrast with current practice, we want to draw out and emphasise the absolute interrelation of discourse and its mode of appearance, and, in doing so, insist that discourses appear in very many modes. Or, to put it differently, all the semiotic modes which are available as means of realisation in a particular culture are drawn on in that culture as means of the articulation of discourses. Of course there may be preferred arrangements of the relations of mode and discourse, and we will draw attention to such instances as they emerge.

As a first larger example, we will look more closely at the domain of 'the house' and of 'living', as it is articulated discursively and textually in everyday practices, such as where and how we live – the kinds of spaces we inhabit, the kinds of things we do in them, the way we 'furnish' them, the way we use spaces in relation to various activities, the aesthetics of such arrangements, etc. We want to insist from the beginning that the semiotic instances in which we are interested – the texts – include the everyday practices of 'ordinary' humans as much as the articulations of discourses in more conventionally text-like objects such as magazines, TV programmes, and so on. We will refer to these 'practically lived texts' just as much as we will refer to the texts of magazines or the plethora of TV programmes. It happens that the latter are more readily disseminated and reproducible here than the former; but all of them are sites where discourses appear.

Our point is that discursive action takes place in, and is articulated in, a multiplicity of practices and a multiplicity of modes, of which lived human social action is one. In the previous chapter we said that a mode is that material resource which is used in recognisably stable ways as a means of articulating discourse – so that some actions in some domains may be entirely mode-like, others may be quite mode-like, and yet other actions may not be highly developed as modes at all.

Let us begin by discussing a magazine, one of very many in Anglophone Western cultures (with the comment that the form of such text-objects, their forms of production and their dissemination, is in itself a fact of major social semiotic significance). The magazine is *Maison Française*, its publication date Summer 1996. The theme of this issue, announced on the front cover (Fig. 2.1), is 'Rêve d'été' – dream of summer. It promises to speak 'du soleil, de l'ombre, de l'eau, de l'air, de blue, du blanc' – of sun and shade, water and air, blue and white. It contains features on such topics as light furniture, natural fibre floor coverings, garden tables, and on 'the pleasures of the shower', 'the charm of the veranda', and 'new timber houses'.

Two colours, blue and white, are present throughout the magazine. Nearly every (double) page contains either of these colours in some noticeable, usually striking form, or has at least a visual reference to water and air – a view of a lake, of the sea, or a strong visual reference to 'light' and 'air' as 'airiness'. The (Mediterranean) house featured has white walls and blue window frames, doors, patio-roofing and swimming pool; advertisements of display furniture, towelling, crockery, cutlery against a blue and white backdrop, in the blue and white interiors of rooms; and the page layout features white and blue backdrops and white or blue lettering.

Colour here takes on the functions of a mode and is used to articulate aspects of a discourse of living. The values attached to light, water, to the outdoors – in short, to a specific social conceptualisation of the natural environment – are brought into everyday living in order to structure it and make it meaningful, whether through the colour of the coffee bowl used at breakfast, of the shower room, of the towel used after the shower, or of the furniture to lounge on or sit at. Colour – this particular selection of colours and opposition of colours, always clear, saturated, sharply articulated – acts as the carrier of discourses about forms of living, about dispositions of human lives, just as the colours of Stephanie's bedroom spoke of what children were thought to be and were expected to become.

This is more than a matter of 'aesthetics' or of 'style', where these are conceived of as relatively tangential to meaning, as 'ornamental' – rhetorical in the negative and trivial sense. Discourse, realised through the mode of colour, expresses and articulates knowledge of why a specific domain of social reality is organised the way it is, how human lives are lived in the house, how they are to be thought about, and of what values – in the widest sense – attach to these ways of living. The linguistic description amplifies this: the blue, for instance, is 'serene yet dynamic' and 'encapsulates, solidifies and underlines the pure and strong architecture of the

Figure 2.1 *Front cover of* Maison Française *(Summer 1996)*

house'. Even though – as we are told – the ownership of the house has recently changed hands, the new owners 'have allowed themselves to be "subjected" to the rhythm of the house', like their predecessors, 'slipping into this house as into a second skin'. The colours organise this rhythm. As a caption next to a picture of one of the bedrooms says, 'The bedrooms do not escape the colours of the house. Nothing does, not even the shower cubicle' (with a picture of that space underneath). The house dictates the 'pace and the manner of living, with bedrooms as small islands atop their steep staircases'. 'Less than a living space, the oblique passage across the patio gives focus to the life of the blue house'... 'yet everyone can find their own corner for privacy (solitude), whether on the veranda, or on the restful rocky spots which spill down to the sea'.

Here we come to a consideration of other modes and their contribution to the articulation of this discourse of 'living': the mode of architecture, which relates more strongly to the discursive practices realised in action, and the issue of the materiality of the house, and of its environment, as expressed in several places, here in the 'rocky resting places', the 'rocky island in the centre of the patio'.

We will discuss these aspects of mode and their interrelation with discursive practice in more detail below, but at this point we wish to draw attention to the potential of colour for articulating discourses. Colour as mode is entirely distinct from language as mode. Even though we regard mode as an abstract organisation, it is the abstract organisation of a specific material drawn into semiosis in a culture through practices of producing dyes (and other colouring technologies) in colours recognised as relevant and meaningful in that culture. Here colour offers semiotic possibilities of a specific kind, for instance the possibility of 'association' with other colours, with other materials (air, rock, wind, sea/water, cloth, etc.), and with other culturally salient aspects ('sun', 'shade') and their meanings in a culture, and at a particular time (this is the summer issue of the magazine, and, as we will show below, seasonality is drawn into semiosis in its own culturally and socially distinctive ways). Colour also offers a specific sensory appeal, via sight and its physiology, and via both the physiological/experiential meanings of colour for humans as biological/ physiological beings and the cultural/experiential meanings of colour – the meanings deriving from specific cultural provenances and physiological/experiential/ emotional effects.

It is at this point that the articulation of (an abstractly existing) discourse in (an abstracted) mode becomes specific to the mode. Not only would a translation into the mode of language, whether as speech or as writing, lose many essential specifics – the specific kind of blue, the sharpness of the contrast, the possibilities of visual associations with other visually represented aspects of shape, texture, material, and with other colours – but it would also create entirely different experiential effects: hearing the word *blue* is not the same as seeing a deeply saturated *blue*. The meaning-associations capable of being set up visually are simply not those which can be set up verbally.

Sense, materiality, mode and discourse

The abstractness of the category of discourse, as much as the abstractness of its discussion in academic contexts, is prone to make us forget that experience is not abstract, ever. Experience is physical, physiological, even though it is of course culturally mediated through culturally given systems of evaluation. In semiosis the materiality of modes interacts with the materiality of specific senses, even though modes are conventionalisations produced through cultural action over time, and therefore abstract in relation to any one particular action. To some extent this sensory directness of modes can lead to an opposite response to that just mentioned. The material qualities of a voice – the 'grain of the voice' for instance – may make us forget the culturally and socially produced character of the voice as mode, as may happen with all of the selections of materials which appear in semiosis. So we might experience a sense that experience is unmediated by culture, that it is direct and individual.

In the magazine's description of this house there are sharp contrasts: of the smoothness of the stones in the rocky outcrop of the patio, and of the rocks 'spilling down' to the swimming pool; of the textures of the vegetation and of the rocks; of the natural and the built environment; of the materials of furnishings, buildings, exteriors, pottery, etc. There are contrasts of shapes and of lines, all expressed, articulated, realised, physically and materially. By contrast, discourse in its abstract conception, as much as mode in its abstract conception, seems to be entirely *immaterial*, not related to the sensoriness of human beings, which consequently has been too often excluded from considerations of semiosis. But even though this view has dominated academic work for a considerable period, perhaps ever since the Enlightenment with its conceptions of rationality separated from the body, it is deluded. A semiotics which is intended to be adequate to a description of the multimodal world will need to be conscious of forms of meaning-making which are founded as much on the physiology of humans as bodily beings, and on the meaning potentials of the materials drawn into culturally produced semiosis, as on humans as social actors. All aspects of materiality and all the modes deployed in a multimodal object/phenomenon/text contribute to meaning.

Several issues need attention here: what modes are used and therefore what materials are invoked, and therefore, what are the senses which are involved? What differential possibilities of perception and cognition are invoked through the uses of different materials and modes? What difference in kinds of meaning is produced in the use of different modes and materials – the kinds of meaning usually referred to as emotive, affective, aesthetic, and the kinds of meaning referred to as semantic, rational, logical, ideational? Two further questions to which attention needs to be given are these: to what extent do specific modes have linguistic analogues or translations, and to what extent (how fully) are the materials which are used articulated as modes? For instance, in relation to the first of these two questions, it is clear that a mode (gesture, colour, taste) may be quite fully articulated and yet not have a correspondingly articulated set of labels in language, spoken or written. Colour may be an example. Whether in the case of *Maison Française* or of *Home Flair* (an English magazine), colour is available as a mode with well-articulated discursive possibilities.

But the range of linguistic terms available to 'translate' them into speech is roughly as we have indicated here. It turns out that the mode of colour is more articulated than are the terms available for translating them into the mode of language. In part at least this also answers the second of the two questions: colour, in each of the magazines, is available as a well-articulated mode for the expression of discursive meanings. These questions represent a largely unexplored semiotic terrain, although attention has increasingly been given to these issues over the last fifteen or twenty years, as in the writings of Howard Gardner (e.g. 1993) and Oliver Sacks (1984).

Comparison of magazine-texts in this area (as of course elsewhere) leaves us in no doubt that discourses are articulated in modes other than speech or writing. An issue of *Home Flair* (November 1997) also focuses on colour. The front cover (Fig. 2.2) highlights four features in the magazine: 'over £5,000 worth of solid pine bedroom furniture to be won'; 'love at first sight: the problems and pleasures of buying a picture postcard cottage'; 'fashionable fabrics: 15 pages of top textiles' and 'cover look: dreaming in colour; a country kitchen with a modern taste'. Here the colour scheme is – as one might predict from the features ('pine furniture', 'picture postcard cottage', 'country kitchen') taken together with the provenance of this magazine, England (not France or Italy) – entirely different from that of *Maison Française*: browns, yellows and oranges dominate, with blues and greens present as subsidiary colours.

A further factor enters, as we suggested above. This is the November issue. Seasonality has not, to the best of our knowledge, so far featured in discussions of discursive arrangements; yet that seems to be the shaping factor here. Seasons have social and cultural meanings: they are discursively organised. The editor's introduction speaks of 'crisp, autumnal nights' with 'a blazing bonfire, baked potatoes and mulled wine', of Guy Fawkes' night and Hallowe'en, which have inspired 'things bright and orange', and of 'rich russets, golds and greens, all synonymous with Sunday afternoon autumn walks ...'. A feature, 'What's New', speaks of the 'full enjoyment of the classic British Winter'. As with *Maison Française*, a whole vast set of practices, of values, a widely ramified aesthetic and value system, is invoked here. And here, too, as in the French magazine, though in totally different articulations, modes other than language realise a set of discourses around living, e.g. through the textures, shapes and colours of objects such as curtain rails and curtains, toasters, fireplaces, furniture, fabrics, and knick-knacks of all kinds. Language-as-writing can translate and articulate only a small part of this.

The potential answer to the earlier questions 'What materials, what modes and therefore what senses?' may provide important clues to the 'take-up' and effectiveness of articulations of discursive meanings in specific modes. In other words, we doubt that language is the most effective mode in all circumstances, both because colour as mode – to take an example – may be able to realise discursive meanings which writing or speech could not, and because some

Figure 2.2 *Front page of* Home Flair *(November 1997)*

meanings may be more readily 'received' in one mode rather than another. In other words, discursive practice in a multimodal environment consists in the ability to select the discourses which are to be 'in play' on a particular occasion, in a particular 'text'. This is the issue of Foucault's theory of discourse (1977; see also Kress 1985; Fairclough, 1989). But more than that, on the other hand, communicational practice consists in choosing the realisational modes which are apt to the specific purposes, audiences and occasions of text-making. This is what we will address under the heading of 'design'. This requires the choice of materials and modes which for reasons of cultural history and provenance, or for reasons of the individual's history, are best able to (co-)articulate the discourses in play at the particular moment. That is, it is a matter not only of organising discourse abstractly considered, but also of organising the realisational modes for the discourses. That involves selecting the material forms of realisation from the culture's existing repertoire, and of selecting the modes which the producer of the text judges to be most effective (whether consciously so or not is not the issue at that point) in relation to the purposes of the producer of the text, expectations about audiences, and the kinds of discourses to be articulated.

In several of the English 'home' magazines that we looked at, the themes of tradition, heritage and aesthetics are brought together to create a mood of nostalgia. 'Centuries ago, meals were cooked on open fires in the middle of the same room where everyone lived, ate, and slept. Today, although much has changed, the kitchen remains at the heart of every household. Here, families gathered ... surrounded by the heavenly aromas of baking and roasting and the scents of freshly picked herbs ... today we have the chance to recreate the authentic country kitchen ...' (*Home Flair*, November 1997: 44). The mode of writing is clearly used to set the tone, to indicate how the other modes and the objects and structures which they articulate are to be read and understood. However, language does not indicate the colour range (on this page a dominant reddish brown, with yellows, greens, oranges, reds, blues, whites); and it is the colour range which is a central factor in creating the specific aesthetic as well as the ideological effects of nostalgia. The same is true for the patterns (turned table and chair legs, check materials, cushions, tablecloths, plates, curtains, textures of pine, linen, enamel, crockery), and of course for the objects themselves (the tables, chairs, dresser, soft furnishings, enamel jugs, pottery mugs, etc.). Each of these, not forgetting the bunch of yellow tulips (in November in the northern hemisphere!) in a jug on the kitchen table, belongs in a recognisable and well-understood set of signs.

The provenance of the signs is foregrounded in every case, whether the country-style carved wooden chairs, the check pattern of the tablecloth or the hatched pattern of the blue and white show plate on the dresser – as it was, in a very different set of discourses, in the house of *Maison Française*, where each item was a designer-produced object, with the name of the designer indicated and the minimalist aesthetic providing the dominant discourse. But the materiality of the mode in which signs are articulated is equally important here: drinking coffee from a pottery mug is not the same experience as drinking coffee from a porcelain cup – a difference due to a different sensory response to the materiality of shape (to touch and sight) and to the materiality of substance (porcelain vs fired clay), to the touch of the lips as much as to the weight of the cup or mug in the hand, and also to the cultural provenance of coffee-mug rather than of porcelain cup.

Discursive practice here lies precisely in the assembling of just these discourses, their articulation in these specific modes and their materialities. Of course, discursive practice is not mere assemblage: as we have said, assemblage entails prior selection, and prior selection entails prior choice. This selection and this choice apply in relation to discourses, to elements in discourses, and to the choice of modes for articulation. Here, in the example of *Home Flair,* for instance, we think that the discourse of aesthetics is articulated in the main through objects-as-mode (furniture, etc.) and through colour-as-mode (the range of colours, around a dominant 'colour core'). Language-as-writing, as we indicated, may be used to provide a frame for interpretation, a particular pointing, what we can call a social/ideological deixis.

Given this semiotic work, discursive practice is always at least reproductive, at one level – the discourses which are in play are reinstantiated in this instance in the text, and the modes used in their articulation are also instantiated. And discursive practice is always also productive and transformative, in that the particular configuration of discourses and their modal articulation inevitably produces a new, changed, transformed arrangement, with effects on each of the contributing discourses, and on each realisational mode.

In other words, the kitchen in this magazine may be stereotypical at one level, and yet in its specific characteristics it will also be like no other kitchen in no other magazine, even in the same broad discursive/ideological arena, and with broadly the same intended audience (the tulips in November may be an accident, a kind of 'punctum' by mistake, while the paper sunflowers on the dresser are 'in keeping', but they are just one instance of this). In a feature 'Choosing the Look' in *House Beautiful* (September 1996: 73–5) the emphasis is on the dining room. One 'look' (pp. 74–5) is closely aligned to the 'look' of the kitchen we have just discussed (Fig. 2.3): the colour range is nearly the same, though the browns tinge into the yellowish rather than the reddish; the furniture is wooden pine, 'country', with turned legs, though less elaborately than in the *Home Flair* kitchen; sunflowers are on the table rather than on the also present wooden dresser, etc.

Ideologically, this room clearly belongs with the *Home Flair* kitchen. Many or all of its discourses are discourses of the kitchen, and so is the modal articulation (colour, objects, materials), though with the absence of the fabrics which are so heavily present in the *Home Flair* kitchen – no tablecloths, no curtains, only covered cushions on the dining chairs. Yet in terms of a specific instance of discursive practice, this text/room, as well as its multimodal representation in two dimensions in the magazine, is distinct from the *Home Flair* room; and this is not, we need to say, because one is a kitchen and the other a dining room. The kitchen has no real evidence of being a kitchen – no stove, no sink, no refrigerator – and the two rooms have the same type of furnishing: either could from that point of view be called 'kitchen' or 'dining room'. *House Beautiful* shows a somewhat plainer, less ornate 'look' than *Home Flair,* and in this small differences lies, we believe, the work – and the slight, incremental effect – of discursive practice.

THE DINING ROOM • ROOM SERVICE •

If your dining room is a neglected corner of the house, you're missing a great opportunity to create a warm, welcoming area that you won't want to save for mealtimes. We've rounded up classic and contemporary looks

CHOOSING THE LOOK

ONTEMPORARY LINES

e, well-designed furniture, pale , bright accessories and bold, rned fabrics combine to create ny, uncluttered feel – the ct setting for long, leisurely meals

expanse of pale wood laminate flooring links ing and kitchen areas in this dual-purpose The simple white scheme is livened up with r coloured chairs and accessories. The laminate g shown here is Birch Planked Pergo Original erstorp Flooring, about £38.20 a sq metre.

2 To add a more formal look to a simply furnished room, the Holst dining table, £225, is teamed with Sloop dining chairs, £49 each, and the elegant Amadeus cabinet, £399. All from Habitat.

3 Natural floorcoverings, wicker and pale wood create a colonial look when teamed with the Cleopatra range of cottons, £10.92 a metre from Montgomery Interior Fabrics. Curtains and furnishings can be made to order.

4 If you're working to a budget, look at dual-purpose conservatory-style furniture. The Farindo wrought-iron, glass-topped table costs £169 and wicker chairs are £75 each. All from The Pier.

5 Focus attention on the dining table with the Aldous floor-standing lamp, £80. Frosted blue and green bottles, tumblers and vases start at £3. All from Bhs.

PULL OUT AND KEEP • PULL OUT AND KEEP •

Figure 2.3 *'Choosing the Look'* (House Beautiful, *September 1996*)

In any case, the articulation of the (let us say) discourse of aesthetics through the modes of colour and of objects leads to a different sensory response than its articulation through language-as-writing. And this different sensory response leads to 'meanings' which are in a significant sense distinct from meanings produced via the articulation of this discourse in language-as-writing. So, for instance, in relation to (the discourse of) aesthetics, two of the magazines – *Home Flair* and *House Beautiful* – make use of the term 'classic': 'the full enjoyment of the classic British Winter' (*Home Flair*, November 1997: 5); and 'her choice of classic English furniture' (*House Beautiful*, September 1996: 46). This is a term in the discourse of aesthetics, and in both instances it is used as such. However, its domain of reference – its semantic/ideological domain as much as its sensory impact – is entirely different from the impact and the domains of the instances discussed.

At the moment we have only hunches as to the longer-term semiotic effect on any individual of this different articulation and experience. One thing we can say is that language is still the mode which is foregrounded in terms of the potentials for analysis and critique, both in academic and in popular discussion, while modes such as colour are not. The possibilities of gaining understanding through forms of analysis are therefore readily available for language and are less so, at this time, for, say, colour.

Ideology, lifestyle and wider social contexts

We have used the term 'ideology' several times now. Our reasons are that we need to be able to distinguish between discourse in our (and others') definitions of it, and the arrangement (choice, selection, ordering) of discourses in texts or text-like objects, or in practices. Such arrangements result in particular ensembles of discourses appearing in texts, producing effects for which we use the term ideology. Practically as well as theoretically we need a means to account for changes in discursive practices. Given our social semiotic perspective, we take the position that such changes have a number of motivations, of which larger-scale social, economic, political and technological practices and changes in practices are one. For us, ideology is a useful and necessary mediating term: mediating in the sense of accounting for arrangements of discourses (and accounting indirectly for changes in discourses as well as in discursive practices) and mediating in the sense of accounting for relations between articulation/realisation (where discourse and mode are both articulatory phenomena) and other social practices, organisation and events.

In our underpinning theory of social semiosis the idea of semiosis as work, as action, is central. There is both a need to account for change in the sets of representational resources, and a possibility for doing so through the action of socially situated individuals in their semiosic action. That is the specific emphasis of the next section in this chapter. We mention it here because it is this which allows us to connect macro-level changes (changes in discourse) with other macro-level changes (changes in economic practice – themselves of course articulated in many instances in a wide variety of discourses and modes), and it is this, also, which allows us to account for changes in discursive practices. The latter are always in the end effects of the action of individuals in social semiosis.

The three magazines which we have used so far are all, in their similar and different ways, embedded in larger economic practices – of course immediately in the practices of advertising and marketing, and hardly less immediately in practices of economic production and consumption. One textual/generic difference between the magazines which we will point to here, even though we will not explore it, is that in the English *Home Flair* and *House Beautiful* there is a nearly total blending of genres which are (still) relatively distinct in *Maison Française*, the genres, broadly, of features and advertising. Both 'Dreaming in Colour' in *Home Flair* and 'Choosing the Look' in *House Beautiful* are entirely blends of feature and advertisement: every item shown is listed with the names of suppliers and an indication of the price. In this respect these magazines have now become very close to being like the sales catalogues of many firms, for instance the catalogue for firms such as IKEA or, in France, FLY, where many commodities are also advertised in settings such as kitchen, bathroom, dining room, study etc. In the French magazine the generic forms are (still) relatively distinct. This may be an effect, of course, of class as much as of national culture, or, as we wish to suggest here, of a mixture of lifestyle, class and national cultural differences.

The shift from a social organisation around class to a social organisation around lifestyle is, semiotically as well as economically and socially, of the greatest significance. The issue is not whether Western post-industrial societies still are or are no longer organised by the social facts of class, or to what extent social class and lifestyle now co-exist and interpenetrate. The issue is that semiotically speaking the culturally dominating paradigm in the public domain is now that of 'lifestyle': it organises advertising and its discourses as much as it is beginning to dominate other social and political domains and their discourses. Semiotically the shift entails a distinct move towards (greater) individuation: that is, the self-definition of individuals through forms of consumption accompanied by an ideological current in which individuation is more intensely emphasised. We say 'an ideological current' because we see this both as ideological rather than as unproblematically 'real', and as a current trend rather than as a yet established, settled arrangement (see Beck, 1999).

The semiotic significance arises from the fact that in a period such as this, with the tendencies – if they have reality – which we have described, individuation is achieved through consumption of commodities as signs, and the pressure towards individuation speeds up the dynamics of semiotic change in discursive practices as much as in modal articulations of discourses. There is pressure on social individuals to differentiate themselves in their individuality through semiotic practices. We are not making the claim that the process is unusual or new; what we are suggesting is that the intensity of the dynamic for change in practices increases the intensity of the dynamic of change in the various articulatory modes, and in the discourses which they articulate. Action is both more intensely and overtly semiotic, and more intensely dynamic. And these factors are interlinked with practices in all domains, at the meta-level and at the micro-level. Articulatory modes which were formerly tangential, marginal, or not fully utilised and developed as modes are being drawn into the centre of semiotic practice. Here they provide new materialities and a more insistent appeal to the sensory/bodily aspects of communication. All these may be effects of this change.

Transformations and the semiotics of action and practices

In their multimodal articulation of multiple and integrated discourses, the magazines we have discussed project not only value systems and forms of aesthetics, but also, as we have shown, forms of practice: whether the practice of chatting in the kitchen, baking, picking herbs freshly; of enjoying the bright, warm, stark or cooling colours and colour-schemes; of traversing a patio and finding companionship in the course of doing that, or seeking solitude on a terrace; or of engaging in autumnal pursuits in the classic British countryside. Yet it might seem from this discussion that such action is either intransitive, self-contained (traversing a terrace, chatting, walking in the countryside) or instrumental, a use of buildings, objects, implements (such as lounging in a chair, making toast with the toaster, etc.) rather than action on things, on people, action with real effects.

In fact we see semiotic action as real action, as work. Work transforms that which is worked on. Action changes both the actor and the environment in which and with which she or he acts. For us this is a point of theory. With reference to the editors of the magazines who, in their (re)arrangements of discourses and modes of articulation, both maintain a certain stability of arrangements and contribute to constant development and change, in discourse as much as in modes, it is an instance of their kind of work.

We say that all social action is semiotic, and that all semiotic action is social; that social action changes both the actor and the 'acted-on' or 'acted-with'. This may seem uncontentious now, as far as traditional traditional textual phenomena are concerned. But we propose to treat all cultural and social products in this fashion. For this to be a plausible approach, we need to show how this is or can be so in relation to materials and modes which in their material stability seem to rule out, to resist entirely, the transformative action of individuals. Yes, we can (re)arrange the furniture in a room, but most of us don't cut up and thereby transform the dining-room chairs we just bought. Is the rearrangement of a room the making of a new sign, as the transformation of existing forms and resources? If all our social semiotic environment is organised in the form of semiotic modes, and therefore as sets of signs with known meanings and regularities of use attaching to them, how can we maintain that we act transformatively in all our actions in semiosis?

Let us look now in more detail at an example of 'practically lived texts'. From the 1970s onward, middle-class families began knocking down walls (or rather, and more usually, paid a builder to do so) in the inner-city houses into which they were beginning to move at that time, whether in the inner-city suburbs of Sydney or of London. It is essential to see this as ideologically and therefore socially, economically, and aesthetically driven. The British terraced house is basically a structure of 'two (rooms) up, two (rooms) down', with various kinds of elaboration on this 'two up, two down' structure developed over the course of the nineteenth century (in somewhat distinctive ways in tropical Singapore, hot Sydney, or cooler London), in finely articulated nuance in relation to class (and income) difference. As with the architects in Amsterdam or Vienna referred to in the previous chapter, precisely articulated notions of social practice and of their value systems – of who did what, where, when – were set in bricks and mortar in the endless rows of such houses in the British Empire (the social and architectural history of the terraced house is well documented, see for example Muthesius, 1982). One of the elaborations of the 'two up, two down' structure was the addition of a 'service section' at the back of the house, in which kitchen and scullery could be accommodated. This elaboration was not merely practical in its effects, but accentuated a distinction between 'front' and 'back', where 'front' was the *public* part of the house, and 'back' the more *private*, with 'front' higher in social status than the back. Hence in such houses, beyond a certain size, the back section was inhabited by the maid, working downstairs in the scullery and kitchen and sleeping upstairs usually in a tiny room also in the back section, built above the back section of the ground floor.

One form of 'middle-class knocking down' reflected the changed relation and valuations of front and back, public and private, high and low status. The ideology of 'living' of the 1970s had begun to stress the possibilities of living outside, even in Britain, and so an opening to the garden, now no longer used for growing vegetables, drying clothes and accommodating an outside toilet, was derived – a glass door or a big window out onto, or better still into, the garden. This shift around, this realignment of the house, a turn through 180 degrees, literally and metaphorically, in the social orientation of values around living, went with or realised a realignment, a shift in the social orientation of the family, and therefore of the house, and amounted to a fundamental transformation through semiotic/ideological/physical action on the house-as-sign. It was accompanied by other social changes of the 1960s and 1970s, such as the vast rearrangement of status hierarchies involving the reconfigurations of the distinction of public and private, and their effects on the relation between adults and adults, and between adults and children in the family structures of these societies.

Thus the knocking down of the wall between kitchen and scullery, for instance, opened a space where the family could, as *House Flair* suggests, hark back to an unspecified past, or gather to 'eat, chat, and even entertain' in the kitchen, whether surrounded by 'heavenly aromas' or not. The opening out to the garden not only allowed in much more light (another aspect of this transformation, again met earlier in Stephanie's room), but also gave a view out into 'nature', and permitted the cook to pick herbs freshly from the obligatory pots of parsley, thyme and chives on the paved back patio, where meals could be had – informally – in the right weather.

The knocking down, ubiquitously, of the wall between the front room and the room behind (in some Victorian houses there was already a partition formed by wooden doors which could be opened) responded in part to different ideological motives but also paralleled the rearrangement of the distinctions of public and private. Motives such as 'larger space', 'lighter', 'airier' rooms, and in general the falling out of the use of certain kinds of formal entertainment ('receiving' visitors in what real estate agents in their written descriptions still call 'reception rooms') which had marked the rigorous framing of public and private, and the shift to informal, less strongly bounded and framed activities, declared the changed discourses of family and the family's relation to the world. In general, all these were signs of the turning away from a focus on the public to a focus on the private (where both domains are of course social/cultural/semiotic constructs). Literally and semiotically, it was a turning away from the public road, the place of public communication, and a turning in to the space of the family, of the house, and of socialised nature, the private garden.

The fact that this movement occurred right across the Anglophone world shows its ideological character, and the significance of public organs of ideological dissemination such as the magazines we focused on earlier. In projecting and proposing a 'lifestyle' they establish a certain stability ('This is how one lives') and give stability to discursive arrangements and their attendant practices. In this they perform a broadly pedagogic function – telling readers what values and practices to adopt, how to think of themselves, who and how to be. Nevertheless, it is the 'family', or those in the family who have the task of ideological/discursive management, which is the agent of implementation of the discursive/ideological projections – 'designs' in our theory – of the magazines.

If the transformative act of knocking down walls is a fundamental remaking of the house-as-complex-sign, of the house-as-text, it has to remain a relatively rare semiotic act even for the most ardent home-improver. Other acts of semiosis transform parts of the sign complex. Social practices in the house are associated with physical spaces: the spaces where the family watches television, e.g. in the kitchen, in the dining room, in the living room; the spaces where meals are had (whether with or without television), e.g. 'informally' in the kitchen, or in a formal space set aside for all meals eaten by all the family together; spaces which are given over to specific purposes such as sleeping, entertaining, study, whether these are integrated into other spaces or not (a study in a corner of a living room). There is also the question of who is entitled to their own spaces, and at what age (provided the space is available) children will have 'their own' spaces; or, if space is not available, the question of how spaces are marked off for each child, and for each adult.

In other words, a house is a highly flexible set of signifiers, available for the constant making of new signs in the transformative acts of social living. It is far from rigidly static and varies with family types in the pace and extent of its dynamic (the degree to which transformations can change structure) as well as historically. It is a set of signs which is constantly transformed. The house signals the social relations and value systems of the family itself as well as its relations with its social group. A visitor may be entertained in the kitchen, a sign of informality, solidarity, intimacy; or in the dining room, if the family has made the decision (and has been able to make the decision) to allocate space in that manner. The decision not to have a large eating space (the house which one of us purchased had at that time a tiny table in the kitchen for eating at, sufficient at most to seat three people uncomfortably, and had no other space for eating) will signal certain social practices and relations, for instance the practice of eating and entertaining in the public spaces of restaurants rather than at home, so that eating other than with the closest family members becomes largely an activity of the public domain.

These transformative actions on the house are closely related, as we stress, to other social practices and value systems. They are (trans)coded in magazines and television programmes of the kind we have discussed as well as articulated in the house through actions and materials – knocking down, reshaping, painting, wall-papering, carpeting, taking carpet out to restore original wooden floors, etc. They are projected in magazines and television programmes, but transformatively implemented, acted out, articulated by individuals, and these actings-out are never just direct implementations, 'copies of the original'. Work of whatever kind is always transformative.

We have here mentioned transformations which might be regarded as taking place at the macro- (or meso-) level of signs. But transformations take place at every level, including the micro-level, and incessantly so. The decision to entertain a friend for dinner in the kitchen is one transformation if last time we entertained her or him in the dining room. To set the kitchen table with a white tablecloth is a transformation if usually we use place-mats, making the informal slightly heightened as a sign of our sense of the friend and of the occasion. To use one set of plates rather than another (if choice is possible) is another transformation. To serve three courses for that meal in the kitchen rather than two or just one is yet another one, etc. (These micro-level decisions are of course based on notions of design, and are productions of these designs as we have already indicated, and as we will discuss further in the chapters following.) But these micro-level discursive actions will lead to changes at the meso-level or at the macro-level. Entertaining in the kitchen may lead to 'We need a larger table in the kitchen', which may lead to 'We can't accommodate a larger table in the kitchen' and 'We need to extend the kitchen'. Changes to the arrangements of rooms fall into this category, as do re-decorations: 'I can't stand that post-modern green and blue in the kitchen anymore'.

Just as the discursive practices of magazine publishing permit change and innovation – within certain limits of a social and economic kind – so the articulations of discursive projections permit the possibility of change, of innovation, of individual expression in transformative action. The house, however rigid as a text/complex set of signs it may seem to be due to its material aspects, is a complex sign which is constantly transformed. Even the shopping bag hastily put down in the hall and the bicycles parked there or hung up in the entrance corridor are transformative actions, and experienced as such. 'Don't turn this into a pigsty, workshop, ...' are expressions precisely of that. As children grow older they may retain their space, but the space may get re-decorated to signal a transition in a phase of the child's life – from toddler to young person, from young person to early teenager.

The decision to turn around the physical, social semiotic orientation of the house from the street to the garden, from facing the public arena to turning in to the private, would no doubt have been utterly shocking to the Victorian social theorist, architect, builder and family. We think that such transformations are in every way akin to the transformations we perform with sets of signs such as the texts of (written) language. When, in the 1960s, rock 'n' roll bands strove for distinctiveness, they did it largely by means of using existing modes – music of course, but also clothing and language. The shock felt at the 'violence done to language' by using an interrogative pronoun as a count noun, as in 'The Who', was every bit as strong as our imagined shock of the Victorian builder and house owner. What is at issue in these transformations is the complex of discourse and modal articulation, in which both are always transformed: hence the shock and at times – when the transformation is too sudden, too great, or too revealing – the outrage.

Semiotic production: articulation and interpretation

Discursive practices are apparent in action, that is, in their articulation in one or more semiotic modes. We can therefore define a text as that phenomenon which is the result of the articulation in one or more semiotic modes of a discourse, or (we think, inevitably, always) a number of discourses. However, semiotic action is not confined to articulation: we treat interpretation as a semiotic action, and do not in principle make any categorical distinction between the two, other than that articulation is production which makes discourses perceivable in a combination of modes, while interpretation is semiotic production which does not make discourses perceivable. This is a negative definition of interpretation, and so we might say, positively, that both articulation and interpretation are forms of semiotic production. Articulation leads to externally evident signs, texts or text-like objects; interpretation leads to signs which are evident (to the interpreter) 'internally'. The signs of articulation are there immediately for perception and interpretation by others; the signs of interpretation are not immediately available to others for their perceptions and interpretations; they form the basis for later articulations, when the transformative actions of the individual in initial interpretation and subsequent (re)articulation have then become apparent. For us it is essential to stress that production is common to both articulation and to interpretation. The general principles of semiosis, of sign-making, are the same in both cases.

Articulation and interpretation are not necessarily combined in one person in relation to a particular mode or set of modes. My knowledge of a language may be sufficient for interpretation of a text, and not sufficient for the production of the same kind of text. My knowledge and capacity in relation to one may be less than my knowledge and capacity in relation to the other. In part this point will be taken up again in the next section and in the next chapter, in relation to the coming together or the coming apart of certain practices, say in relation to certain professions – moves of de-skilling, re-skilling and multi-skilling.

Certain texts are oriented towards interpretation, at least immediately; other texts are oriented towards production. 'Home' magazines are designed for production as interpretation; the cookery recipe and the do-it-yourself magazine are designed for production as articulation. Both articulation and interpretation rest on knowledge, though what the articulator needs to know differs from what the interpreter needs to know. The articulator needs to have precise knowledge about modes and the possible realisations in modes of the discourse projected in (the designs of) the magazines. However, texts always demand action as a response, whether of interpretation or of articulation or both. Our example of the house is an instance of a text which demands constant interpretation and articulation.

A visitor coming to stay in a house makes the point of interpretation most clearly. He or she needs to learn 'how the house operates', 'how the house works' at a number of levels. The 'owners' of the house are constantly (re)articulating the house: living in a house is an active process, in which the house is continuously transformed. 'Owners' are involved in a continuous action of interpretation and articulation: changing the wallpaper here; shifting the bed there; putting carpets in this room so that it might function differently; with 'knocking down'/'building on' being instances at the extreme end of this range. Children frequently articulate and interpret 'their' house very differently from how their parents do, to the constant irritation of both. It would be an interesting exercise to trace the chain of interpretation/articulation of a house over its history, and see how the house-as-complex-sign mirrors or articulates the social movements of its history. This is treating the house as a communicational entity, which seems appropriate within a multimodal view of social semiosis. Such a history would be a rich history of discursive practices over the period of existence of the house – from the layer on layer of paint and wallpaper on doors and walls, to doors blocked up and broken through.

Hierarchies of practices of articulation and interpretation

The fact that different kinds of knowledge are implied in practices of articulation and interpretation finds its clearest expression in the semiotics of work and of professional practices. 'Home' magazines (unlike do-it-yourself magazines) are not meant as a text for articulation – except for certain kinds of do-it-yourself work – precisely because the reader of the magazine is not meant to have the requisite knowledge, and perhaps predominantly because she or he is meant to engage the services of someone who has that knowledge, whether the interior designer, the landscape gardener or the owner of the furniture store, all of whom advertise in or support the magazine precisely for that reason.

There is a further reason for the solidification and reification of complexes of practices, and that is that all action, all practice, rests on an understanding, a knowledge of modes. Speaking a language rests on a knowledge of that language; playing a game of soccer similarly rests on a knowledge of (the 'rules' of) the 'language' of that game; making a chair rests on knowledge about the mode (design principles) of chairs. Whether I choose to accept such a distinction and division depends on a number of factors. I might never employ a landscape gardener, in the absolutely confident knowledge that I – and only I – can design and 'articulate' the garden of my desire; but my neighbour might feel absolutely daunted by the magnitude and the complexity of the task of design, or by that of articulation. Other factors are less individual and more socially regulated. Perhaps I belong to a social group where it is just not 'done' not to have an interior designer, never mind someone to do my hair. I might be in a profession which has absolutely clearly delineated framings of what I can and what I cannot do. 'Demarcation lines', whether in professions, trades or 'private lives', rest on such framings.

At any one period certain of these couplings of practices can come undone, and new couplings can come into being; certain aggregations are unmade and others are newly made. Where practices are tightly framed, hierarchies of practices are likely to develop. Production of a film in the 'classical' Hollywood fashion is an example par excellence, with clearly delineated practices and roles in which, for instance, the director instructs the cinematographer, who in turn instructs the gaffer (the chief lighting technician), while both cinematographer and gaffer also lead their own teams which can be quite large and have a strict division of labour, in which, for instance, the cinematographer will leave the actual operation of the camera to the camera operator, who, in turn, will leave adjusting the focus to the 'focus-puller', loading the film in the camera's magazine to the 'clapper-loader', and so on. Whether the producer or the director is at the top of this hierarchy depends on the context, with traditional Hollywood practice favouring the producer, and European art film the director. What was never in question, however, was the fact of hierarchy.

Multimedia production, by contrast, is unmaking this particular aggregation of discrete practices, and favours multi-skilling, complex practice, which is now not seen as an 'aggregation' but as one integrated practice. If film-making demonstrates specificity of skilling, the totally different arena of pedagogy, contemporary institutionalised education, provides an example of de-skilling, at least in some Anglophone countries. Formerly, in the English tradition, the teacher was in control of curriculum and of its shape to a very large degree; he or she was in control of pedagogic practice in the classroom, as well as being in charge of assessment and evaluation. This aggregation of practices in one person is now being unmade by currently potent ideological and political forces, and teachers are seen as 'delivering' (the newly fashionable metaphor is significant) a curriculum designed elsewhere without the teacher's input, and increasingly tight control is exercised over the mode of 'delivery', the pedagogic practice in the classroom, as well as over assessment and its forms. This de-skilling is, in our terms, taking from teachers the task of design, and is limiting their potential for action to the field of 'delivery' only, a circumscribed form of production, where before he or she was in control of design, of discursive arrangements in the form of curricular content, of production as pedagogic practice, and of practices of evaluation.

Such processes of multi-skilling and de-skilling are the effects in social and economic life of larger-scale economic and ideological shifts. They have semiotic consequences at every level, whether in the shaping of what counts as forms of knowledge in 'disciplines' or 'subjects', or in the existence or decline of professions and trades, or in the appearance, development and availability of clearly understood and articulated semiotic means – the representational modes. They have effects beyond this, in terms of the shaping of social subjects, and the possibilities of being social actors.

The field of discursive practice is social and therefore historical, and cannot be understood without a sense of the historical/social contingencies of the arrangement and configuration of practices and modes. Nor can we hope to understand fully the shaping and the availability of modes and discourses without a clear sense of the embeddedness of semiosis in the social, and of its historical shaping. In short, what we are describing in this chapter and in those which follow is both the principles of social 'semiosis as such', and at the same time of semiosis as it is at this time, in this place, on this occasion. We describe the principles of human social semiosis, but we stress that what are common principles have very different articulation at different times and in different places.

At the same time this is not an attempt to suggest that all is fluid and that nothing is (ever) fixed in the field of social semiosis, that we cannot, either as humans in the social practices of interpretation and production, or as academic analysts in the process of description, point to semiotic arrangements of known possibilities and limitations. It is to say that we are talking about configurations at this time, in a field which is subject to constant human social action.

3 Design

Design in the contemporary period

The term 'design' is currently hugely fashionable. Whenever an idea becomes so ubiquitous that it has entered common parlance to such an extent it is time to ask why. Why is this idea everywhere? Why does it pop up in the most unlikely places? And in particular, why am *I* using this word, this idea? Am I simply caught up in a trend?

Fashions always speak of something real, which may not, however, be quite on the surface of the debate, there for all to see. In the context of a book on multimodality, one answer to the questions we have just posed seems ready to hand: it is the fact of multimodality itself which needs the notion of design. If the awareness of multimodality, and of its move into the centre of theoretical attention in communication and representation, is a recent phenomenon, as we suggest it is, then the emphasis on and interest in the concept of design is, we think, at least in part a consequence of that.

To explain. In an era when monomodality was an unquestioned assumption (or rather, when there simply was no such question, because it could not yet arise), all the issues clustering around the idea of design – a deliberateness about choosing the modes for representation, and the framing for that representation – were not only not in the foreground, they were not even about. Language was (seen as) the central and only full means for representation and communication, and the resources of language were available for such representation. Where now we might ask 'Do you mean language as speech or as writing?', there was then simply 'language'. Of course there was attention to 'style', to the manner in which the resources of 'language' were to be used on particular occasions. And of course there *were* other modes of representation, though they were usually seen as ancillary to the central mode of communication and also dealt with in a monomodal fashion. Music was the domain of the composer; photography was the domain of the photographer, etc. Even though a multiplicity of modes of representation were recognised, in each instance representation was treated as monomodal: discrete, bounded, autonomous, with its own practices, traditions, professions, habits.

By contrast, in an age where the multiplicity of semiotic resources is in focus, where multimodality is moving into the centre of practical communicative action and, though much more slowly, of theoretical attention, and in which it is becoming, palpably, a fact of the everyday communicational life of post-industrial societies, the question 'What mode for what purpose?' has become the central one. In the era of multimodality semiotic modes other than language are treated as fully capable of serving for representation *and* for communication. Indeed language, whether as speech or as writing, may now often be seen as ancillary to other semiotic modes: to the visual for instance. Language may now be 'extravisual'. The very facts of the new communicational landscape have made that inescapably the issue.

There are many other reasons. One has to do with what we might call 'the spirit of the age'. The era of late modernity is, by common consent, regarded as a period of fragmentation, of disparateness, of dispersion. We would not expect representational practices to be immune from this phenomenon. In an earlier period, that of seeming monomodality, representation was seen as coherent, as integrated, and as cohesive, as a reflex of social arrangements and practices which were similarly cohesive and stable. In the domain of work and of the professions, for instance, 'lines of demarcation' were clear and were kept clear (and conflicts were precisely about ensuring that the lines, the boundaries, were clear, hence the prevalence then of 'demarcation disputes'). Mass media production processes were an example of that. The reporter reports, the sub-editor sub-edits, the picture editor selects the pictures, the typesetter sets the pages of the paper, and so on. The practices of each profession, journalist, sub-editor, picture editor, typesetter, are clearly understood and follow well-established practices. In such contexts design is not (seen as) a necessary concept, because 'scripts' exist which are stable, and the stability of these scripts is supervised even when the scripts themselves are never made overt. Most trades prided themselves on the saying – adapted to the trade – that 'journalists (furriers, tailors, teachers) are born, not made', naturalising the scripts. Or else, design was seen to exist, but at a different, hierarchically *higher* institutional level: the editorial group might decide to change the house style; they had the right to (re)design (aspects of) the paper, and of the practices fundamental to its production. The age of desktop publishing and website design has blurred such lines of demarcation, and in many cases has already done away with them altogether.

The scripts underlying traditionally demarcated practices tended to be invisible. Their emergence as an issue of theoretical debate (sometime in the late 1960s and in the 1970s) coincided with the increasing insecurity of their existence. By the 1980s the notion of a script, just like the notion of genre (Van Dijk and Kintsch, 1983; Cope and Kalantzis, 2000), had become a central theoretical concern, reflecting, in the case of genres just as much as in the case of scripts, the phenomenon of the increased instability and fragmentation of these structures. Theoretical debates on genre and on the stability of genres became most insistent at the very moment when the phenomenon itself had begun to become highly problematic.

Today, by contrast, the notion of design is foregrounded: the organisation of what is to be articulated is overtly an issue. As we have said, the previously secure 'scripts' have become and are becoming unstable, and new practices for which no scripts as yet exist are coming into being. Previously distinct practices, the domains of distinct professions, the clear boundaries, all of these have begun to unravel. New domains of practice are in the process of being constituted, and new sets of practices are emerging or will undoubtedly emerge in time; and with these new practices will emerge new, not yet consolidated professions. The practitioner in this new domain now has to take a multiplicity of decisions, in relation to a multiplicity of modes and areas of representation which were previously the domain of discrete professions and their practices.

The former boundaries between certain sets of professions and trades have become weakened, permeable, or have, in many cases, disappeared under the pressure of quite new representational arrangements. Formerly, professions established themselves in relation to *one mode*, or around what was seen as one mode, and developed their practices around that. The issue of choice did not arise in this context. Instead of choice there was competence, and competent practice in relation to one mode – whether that was the mode of writing, as in the production of a film script for instance; of image production, as in cinematography; of acting, or of musical composition, to name but some of the distinct competencies that traditionally go into the production of films. In the case of industrial modes of semiotic production such as film production, one person then *integrated* the various practices of a group of professionals into one coherent performance – the conductor of the orchestra (from the mid-eighteenth century onwards), or the editor (and the editorial team) of the newspaper, or the director of the film. Digital technology, however, has now made it possible for one person to manage all these modes, and to implement the multimodal production single-handedly.

The previous monomodal world and its arrangement gave rise to the hierarchies needed for the implementation of 'orchestrated' performance: conductor, leader of the orchestra, first violin, etc. The new arrangements have, as contemporary management jargon has it, 'flattened' that hierarchy. The previously monomodally conceived arrangements (one profession deals with one mode and in that profession there are hierarchically differentiated practices and jobs) gave rise to highly articulated and stable design practices (scripts) in relation to the use of one mode, and, of necessity, to practices for the integration of these discrete practices, when they were joined with other discrete practices. The new multimodal arrangements have not yet given rise to new stable arrangements: the new 'scripts' are yet to be written. The fact that contemporary management everywhere, whether in semiotic or in industrial processes, is subject to the same forces, indicates that this phenomenon is deeply ramified in larger-scale economic and social changes.

When practices, habits and traditions persist and come to be closely supervised, two directions might be taken: they may remain inexplicit, implicit, passed on by osmosis, or by the 'mimicking' of observed practices (the professional common sense will then be as we said above: 'You can't teach creative writing', 'Journalists are born, not made', etc., both the subject of fierce debates in the 1970s and early 1980s) or they may be made explicit, articulated, formulated as overtly stated rules or as examples of 'best practice'. 'Cookery' as a social practice took the latter route sometime in the eighteenth and early nineteenth centuries, with the emergence of the first cookery books. In each case the practices exist as 'scripts', either held implicitly by those who are accomplished practitioners, or made overt and available in explicitly stated form, as instructions for production from design.

As with any semiotic practice, the semiotic means involved in design practice may become formulated in terms which are increasingly generalised, increasingly abstracted from the (repeated) instances of the practice, that is, they may become formulated as 'grammar-like' sets of rules. 'Grammars' of design, like the grammars of semiotic modes, may remain at the level of 'habit', or they may be brought into consciousness and deliberateness as overt, codified prescriptions. Whether this happens or not is a historical/cultural matter. What is or becomes 'elevated' into formally codified grammar (for instance the rules of writing, as *style* or as *genre*; the rules of musical composition, as *script*, or *score*; the rules of cooking, as *recipe*) or what is left as implicit and yet well understood (for instance patterns of jazz improvisation, or the 'rules' of home cooking) are matters of the social, and of the politics of social evaluation, of aesthetics, of 'taste', and relate to larger-level social trends and to the ideologies and politics of particular societies, and of particular periods – they are the stuff of the histories of semiotic practice.

At the moment Western, post-industrial societies are in a period of profound transition, in which formerly stable semiotic (and social, professional, institutional) arrangements and framings are coming undone, or are quite deliberately being disassembled, while new assemblings are, as we suggested, also emerging. We have already mentioned teaching as an example of the move from the assemblage of complex practices in one profession – where it seemed like a single practice – to its dis-articulation. Teaching, in England, has over the last eighty years or so been a profession in which the teacher had (relative) control over the shaping of curriculum, and over the pedagogic practices involved in teaching. At the moment this complex is being dis-assembled: more and more, the curricular content is being centrally prescribed, and the role of the teacher is becoming one of retailing that centrally produced content.

With the increasing availability of electronic technologies, and its promises of 'more effective' teaching, this process will accelerate in the near future. The new and the planned 'learning centres' will not have teachers in that older, now still recognisable form. 'Facilitator' is the vogue word which may more nearly describe the new role. At the same time, we need to be aware of the social and historical specificity of these arrangements. No teacher in France (or Germany, or Greece) would, during that same period, have assumed that they should have control over curricular content and structure. These matters are historical, social, contingent. Nevertheless, teaching, in England, is moving from being multi-skilled to becoming specialised. The elements of significant design still adhering to the role of teacher are diminishing. On the other side, as an example of the move in the opposite direction, stands (print) journalism. Here a relatively specialised profession, based on the mode of writing (and increasingly on that of image), is undergoing a change in the other direction. In many contexts, reporting, writing, (sub)editing, layout, publishing, are all merging into a single new practice, through the availabilities and affordances of electronic technologies.

In other words, the process does not move uniformly in the direction of dis-articulation. In the case of industrial semiotic production processes such as newspaper production, movie production and the symphony orchestra, it moves towards re-articulation and integration. In the case of traditionally independent professions (in certain countries), such as teaching, the law, medicine, etc., it moves towards dis-articulation. It is instructive to consider such cases in detail and to reflect on the causes for these dis-articulations and re-articulations. All are bound up, even if at first puzzlingly, with the move from the monomodal representational world (think of the figure of the mid to late 1950s pop singer) to the multimodal representational world of the present (think of Michael Jackson). New semiotic, social, political, institutional arrangements are beginning to take shape, and are quite knowingly being shaped. This process is extending and encompassing (engulfing, if you take an apocalyptic view) more and more of the formerly settled semiotic practices. One result is the foregrounding of design: we might say that we are living in a new age of design.

Coupling and uncoupling of semiotic practices: monomodality and multimodality

Many readers of this book (it is a generational matter, as we have pointed out) will understand our argument about the unmaking and unravelling of previous semiotic, social and professional arrangements well enough in terms of their own professional working experience. For one of the authors of this book the issue of 'demarcation' was brought home very sharply indeed when early in a different kind of working life he 'overstepped the mark'. The occasion was one in which his foreman challenged him about one aspect of his work. In response he started on an explanation with 'I thought I would ...' only to be cut off crisply with 'You're not paid to think'. The boundary he had overstepped was that between design and execution: his role was to execute a design, and certainly not to remake the design itself. At that time (in October 1958, to be reasonably precise), those boundaries were clear: if you were a foreman you might indulge in some 'redesign'; if you were a lowly (young and immigrant) worker you most certainly would not.

In the meantime the world has changed somewhat. In Australia, where the above exchange took place, the mid-1980s saw far-reaching and trade-union led dismantling of these boundaries, for the sake of efficiencies of new workplaces, in the name of 'multi-skilling'. Since then that process has swept across the Anglophone post-industrial world. The point is important, for we want to insist that what look like 'merely semiotic' practices are never just that, but are always tied into much wider, more far-reaching, more widely ramified structures. In this section we will explore this interrelation of institutional/professional practices with semiotic practices in more detail.

Design, we suggested in the previous section, is the organisation of what is to be articulated into a blueprint for production. In that definition the task of the designer is seen as 'architectural': the shaping of available resources into a framework which can act as the 'blueprint' for the production of the object or entity or event. The cookery book is about design; the cooking from the book is not, though the person hosting a dinner party can expend their design energies in small modifications ('Yes, I always like to add some coriander, it just gives it a lift') or in other aspects of the event. The architect who designs the blueprint/plans for a house is a designer; the builder who comes along to 'produce' it should, ideally, not be a designer, but someone who fully reads and understands the printed plans and needs no further assistance in building from them – without change.

The example on which we wish to focus just now is that of an (actual) science teacher – one year qualified – who is teaching a series of lessons on blood circulation. This 'unit of work', comprising four lessons, is not designed by (let us call him) David. 'Blood circulation' is a topic within the science curriculum, as prescribed in the National Curriculum in England. It exists as a topic in various designs: as a sketched topic in the National Curriculum; as a topic in textbooks designed by commercial publishers for this curriculum; and as a topic for the grade he is teaching (a class of 13–14 year olds). It also exists in the practices and the traditions of this school's Science Department, both in the form of advice, of 'core' practices, and of materials: printed, 3D and others.

In other words, major aspects of the curriculum are delineated and even prescribed in quite significant detail. This might suggest that this teacher's role is simply that of executor, or of producer. However, he remains responsible in a significant way for 'the organisation of that which is to be articulated', and this is due, largely, we think, to two factors: first, to the facts of multimodality, and second, to a more general principle of semiosis.

We will take the second point first. One assumption of the monomodal communicational world is that the move from design to production is simply one of instantiation or realisation. In other words, a design is held to be specific to such an extent and in such detail that no decision of any significant kind is left to the producer. Examples might be, in some versions of this, the performance of a piece of classical music (as contrasted with the freedom of the jazz improvisation); the architect's design and the builder's execution of the design; the design of a car and its manufacture; and so on. However, the general principle of semiosis which we adopt is that every act of realisation involves processes of transformation. For one thing, it involves a shift of a modal kind, from a general schema (realised in one mode) to its instantiation in another mode or modes. That process of *transduction* is itself transformative.

Putting it crudely, a blueprint is not the house, however detailed the former may be. This is where the current preoccupation with 'quality control' stems from: the car manufacturer of course has to accept transduction, but wants to keep transformative action to the absolute minimum. And yet we know that some cars are 'duds' from the moment they leave the production line. The extension of the notion of quality control from this domain to nearly all others (teaching, publication, the prison service, hospitals, religion, etc.) is, in this context, *the* interesting phenomenon. For another thing, every act of realisation, from design through to production, involves choices, even in a monomodal conception of the world.

In the case of the science teacher, David may be intending to articulate a particular curricular design (a discourse of the body and its textual structures) in speech; but that leaves open an unlimited number of choices. These include the rhetorical/epistemological position that he chooses to adopt: 'This is the case, and here is a demonstration to show you', versus 'Here is a textbook; it is an authoritative source of knowledge; it tells you what it is like', or 'You know from your own experience what this domain of science is like – you've seen mould growing on your sandwiches when you forgot to take them out of your lunchbox'. (These are referred to as 'rhetorical frames' in Kress *et al.*, 2000.) After this initial semiotic decision, in itself of great consequence for what a scientist is or will strive to be (or, an epistemologically driven decision, with rhetorical/semiotic consequences), a whole range of choices have to be made by her/him, which are about the ultimate instantiation or articulation, the ultimate performance/production of this lesson.

As a question of *design* this involves issues such as what *modes* to use for what segments of the curricular content; how to arrange the content, for instance whether to devise a (largely) sequential structure for it; how to arrange the ensemble of modes in the structure; and, as we said, the initial decision as to the rhetorical *and* epistemological starting point. In this sequence of lessons, the teacher chose the approach of 'this is the case in nature and here are a series of different illustrations of this'. To give an indication of the overall shape of this design we describe its actualisation here, in part, over one lesson. The modes involved were the visual, as image; language, largely as speech, but, in some small part, also as writing, in the form of 'labels' both on the drawn diagram on the blackboard and in a textbook used in the lesson; gesture; the teacher's body (in the space of the classroom); and a physical, material model.

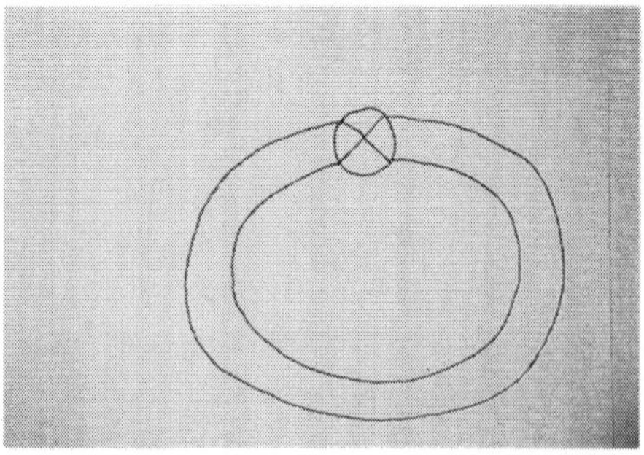

Figure 3.1 *Image on the whiteboard*

Not all of these were co-present at all times, but several of them were always involved. The manner in which the lesson unfolded was as follows: the teacher had drawn a circle on the whiteboard, with an outer and an inner edge (*see* Fig. 3.1), to indicate a tube-like entity (mode: visual image). This was on the board when the students came into the room. Once the class had settled, the teacher, who had stood perfectly still (mode: body in space), walked deliberately across the podium, in front of the board, turned (mode: body in space) and, halfway back, began to speak (mode: language as speech). His talk concerned the diagram: what it stood for, namely, a highly abstracted image of the path of the blood's circulation around the body, with an abstract image element indicating the heart as pump. He proceeded to make the image more complicated by adding a second, smaller circle to the top (mode: image), a second loop which, he explained, showed the blood's path more accurately: around the body, to the head, and back to heart and lungs (*see* Fig. 3.2).

In elaborating the newly complex model in speech, he used gestures (mode: gesture) to make signs indicating the pumping action of the heart (rhythmically

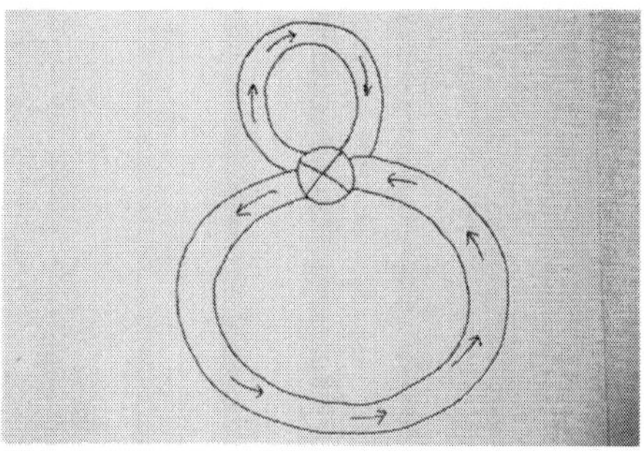

Figure 3.2 *Adapted image on the whiteboard*

Figure 3.3 *Teacher manipulating model of the human body*

pushing his semi-raised arms against his body), and in repeating the account of the blood's circulation, using the diagram, he both used his hands to indicate the motion of the blood (mode: gesture) and at the same time wrote names as labels on parts of the diagram: 'The blood moves around the body, from the heart to the *lungs*, to the small *intestine*, to the *cells*, to the ...' (mode: language as writing). When the diagram had been fully articulated and labelled, he lifted a plastic model of the upper part of a human torso on to the bench in front of him, and, in taking apart the model (mode: model), he stood behind the model, establishing a parallel, so to speak, between his actual, real body and the plastic non-real, regularised body: the model-body as a projection of the real body (*see* Fig. 3.3).

He provided spoken labels (mode: speech) of the parts as he took them from the model (mode: model) and indicated with hands and fingers (mode: gesture) how the blood would move in and around various parts of the model. In this sequence/structure, as we have indicated it so far, it can be seen how different modes are brought together and orchestrated by the teacher, with different modes acting as the major 'carriers' of content at different times and with the modes always drawn in to the semiotic ensemble for quite specific representational/communicational support. At the conclusion of this lesson sequence, David picked up a textbook which had several pages devoted to blood circulation. He pointed to a diagram in the book and then read from the book.

The (two) boundaries of design

What of this sequence/structure had been designed and what not? Our response is that it is not possible to say just from witnessing and describing the lesson. Had we had David's lesson plan, we would have been able to see what was designed – which modes had been deliberately selected, which were to be foregrounded, what the overall sequence was to be. As it is, we must infer from performance/production back to design. But we might suppose, nevertheless, that not all the features of this production had, in fact, been 'designed'. Do we assume, for instance, that gestures-as-mode would have featured in his lesson-plan/design? Do we assume that the precise moments of the arm-pumping action would have been indicated in the design, the 'score' of the lesson? We might assume that the stages and their sequence would have been pre-designed, and that the foregrounded modes might have been indicated, though perhaps not all of these – image, yes; body, perhaps not; gesture, probably not; model, yes; image and writing in the textbook, yes.

All this draws attention to several crucial points about the border between design and production: there need not be, in fact there is unlikely ever to be, a full specification of all of the elements of the eventual production; and there is unlikely to be a full specification of their orchestration. Even in a situation where the teacher's actions and practices are seemingly heavily circumscribed (in England, at least, relative to previous decades), this circumscription captures only parts of what is in fact finally produced/performed. Does this point to the absence of (fully) developed grammars in the area of social practice, to an absence of a grammar of design? Well, maybe yes, and maybe no. Clearly a lesson plan, if demanded, or if made, can encompass modes and structures, though foregrounded modes might actually remain quite invisible even to the maker of the lesson plan: they are 'naturally there'. She or he would not state that they were 'using speech', and the model torso, for instance, might be treated, not as means of communication, but as a 'teaching aid'.

Even so, what is or is not a formally, officially acknowledged mode in a given domain of practice can change over time. Gesture may not, at present, be recognised as a mode in the domain of teaching. But once the psychologist's expertise on 'body language' is drawn into the training of teachers, as it already is in the training of interviewers, interviewees, appraisers, etc., gesture, too, will become more codified. Yet, despite ever-tightening prescription, that which is collected up by 'grammars' of various kinds will always only ever be a fraction, sometimes quite small, of that which appears in performance/production. In our next example we will discuss this question in part in relation to the grammar of writing.

Of course, David had the possibility of other designs: there was no need necessarily for the image on the whiteboard. The fact that he started with that image was an effect of his epistemological/pedagogic decision to begin this 'unit of work' with a high degree of sparse abstraction and work from there both towards ever greater complexity and ever greater realism – until the very end, when he turns to use the textbook, to anchor the knowledge he has developed in its canonical expression.

But given the degree of curricular prescription within which he is working, and even given his epistemological/rhetorical starting point, there was no requirement for him to start with the sparse abstraction of the image of the circular tube. He could have started with the canonical form of knowledge of the textbook; or he could have started with the plastic model. However, within his epistemological/rhetorical framework he could not, we believe, plausibly have started with his own body as the site of demonstration and explanation. He could have made much greater use of the mode of writing, relegating image or 3D model very much to secondary, backgrounded status. And he could have varied the sequential structuring in a number of ways: moving, for instance, from linguistic description to exemplification with the model, and from there to the abstraction of the circle. All these choices of course imply a somewhat different rhetoric and with that some variation within the epistemological position that he has adopted. Each implies a differing pedagogical relation to his audience. But all of these could have been accommodated within his overall epistemological, rhetorical, pedagogical and curricular framework.

One real limitation to his possibilities of choice lies, or lay, within his awareness of what resources are, or were, actually available to him. Here we move to that other boundary of design – the boundary between resources and design. The boundary between design and production is, we said, blurry: usually designs underspecify elements and structures relative to what is to be produced/performed. This is so even in the case of an architect's design of a house, where, depending of course on the particular case, vast ranges of decisions may be left to the builder; though we also assume that there are cases where design is fully specific – in the case of the car assembly plant, or similar high tech instances – hence the concern with quality assurance. At the boundary of resources and design this issue emerges in a related yet distinct form: only those resources which are officially recognised, which are visible as communicational and representational resources, whether highly abstract, such as 'discourses', or entirely materially concrete, such as the materials for making a wall in a house, can become subject to (conscious) design. Semiotic modes which are not in the official, public inventory of modes of a culture or a domain of practice, cannot be drawn into the process of design. Only recognised modes are available as elements for the design process. Similarly, only recognised structures and sequences (syntagms), whether as 'script' or as 'genre', are available to the design process. In the case of David's lesson, this then raises the question of where the other elements and the other scripts come from. Clearly, they are 'there': the gestures are there, the sequencing of modes is clear, once we attend to it; and, moreover, we assume that these 'invisible' elements and structures are understood – even if not in full awareness – by those to whom they are communicated.

For us it suggests that out of the semiotic modes which exist in any one culture only some are officially recognised and therefore available to design processes. These modes are (likely to be) highly developed – with an awareness by members of that culture of their grammar-like organisation. Other modes are not recognised, or are recognised only in relation to certain specific domains, or are semi-recognised. These modes may be well developed, that is, quite fully articulated as semiotic resources, or they may be less so. Similarly with scripts and the rules of genre. Clearly, David can draw on available scripts which are not consciously present for design, in this domain of practice: those involving the semiotic mode of gesture, of the use of his body in space, perhaps in part that of image. What then can be 'designed' (rather than created in the process of the actual, physical production of the semiotic object or event) varies from instance to instance – not haphazardly, but in accord with cultural regularities involving the visibility and recognition of the resources available for design. A discussion such as ours here may have the effect of changing this visibility: for instance, it may be that teacher training courses might include focus on the mode of bodily action. That would bring teaching closer to a domain of practice such as acting, or performance in other fields, in which bodily action is visible, recognised and available for design.

It may be that we can treat the design process as that process which acts deliberately, with awareness, on visible, recognised, 'available' resources in a particular domain, in order to make the blueprint of that which is to be produced. This makes design always contingent: contingent on domain of practice, contingent on the specific stage in a long chain of design-production, where at any point the implementer of a design can become a designer in respect to a particular facet of the productive process.

Grammars for design

We turn now to examine this question of the regularities of design from a slightly shifted perspective. We are aware that design has to be discussed in relation to a specific domain of practice; in relation to what the resources available for design are; and in relation to the regularities which surround this, both in terms of the modes involved, and in terms of design practice. Design practices, operating over extended periods, and in periods of stability, give rise, not only to the regularities of design itself, but also to the specific use of the modes involved in the design. That is, modes become shaped in response to *discourse*, where discourse itself is the effect of the socially shaped design practices. Here we want to discuss these issues in relation to two examples: one a small card, the size and shape of a credit card, which came (as one of three) inside a leather purse; and the other, revisiting an example from the previous chapter, the pages of two 'home' magazines, one French, one English. We will start with the latter, and investigate the matter of colour in relation to the question of mode and the question of the available resources, and of their shape.

As we pointed out, both magazines explicitly declare their interest in colour. The French magazine, *Maison Française*, in its summer issue has as its theme, stated on the front page (Fig. 2.1), 'Rêve d'été' ('Summer Dream') and it is about 'choosing well': 'Bien choisir: des meubles mobiles, des tapis végétaux, des rotins malins, des tables de jardin' ('Choosing well: lightweight furniture, natural fibre floor coverings, garden tables') and 'living well': 'Bien vivre: les plaisirs de la douche, le charme des vérandes, les nouvelles maisons en bois' ('Living well: the pleasures of the shower, the charm of verandas, and new timber houses'). And it speaks 'du soleil, de l'ombre, de l'eau, de l'aire, du bleu, du blanc' ('of sun and shade, water and air, blue and white'). *Home Flair* has as its theme – its 'cover look' – 'dreaming in colour, a country kitchen with a modern taste'. Here we focus, initially, on the French magazine's engagement with *bleu* and *blanc* (in the context of its other stated interests). In one feature in the magazine, 'Le Bleu du Ciel' blue is the dominant colour: 'Entre ciel et mer une couleur s'impose tout naturellement: le bleu. Serein mais dynamique, il encadre, relie, souligne l'architecture pure et dure de cette maison ...' (p. 131) ('Between sky and sea one colour imposes itself naturally, blue. Serene yet dynamic, it frames, connects and emphasises the pure and hard architecture of this house ...').

Our question is: 'Is colour a mode?' That is, is it semiotically organised, is it a regularised means of representation (in the way sound-as-music, for instance, is)? Does it have a cultural history which has made it into a representational resource? What are its regularities, and how might they be described? Another of our questions can be answered straight away: we are in a specific, specialised domain of practice – that of advertising/publishing/(marketing) – with its clear aesthetic requirements and values (of course, in our scheme, aesthetics can be seen to be explicable through a conjunction of the concepts of mode, design and discourse).

In linguistics, one of the formal tests for establishing whether there are regularities is to see if there are irregularities. That is, do members of the culture (or, in this case, of the specialised domain of practice) recognise a rule that has been broken. The test derives from Noam Chomsky's distinction, made in his *Syntactic Structures* (1957), between grammatical and non-grammatical 'strings', well-formed and not well-formed utterances. It is clear, on this criterion, that there can be, and are, ill-formed colour structures, that the colours which co-occur across a page (or a double page spread, or a whole feature article) obey 'rules' of collocation, of what can appropriately go with what.

In the French magazine the *bleu* goes with *blanc* (in various shades of the *bleu*) and with shadings of (off-) white and green. Colour here has a textual function. It forms a cohesive device across the eight pages of this feature article, providing cohesion (and *coherence*) every bit as clearly and as strongly as do the cohesive devices of lexis in language. The text of the magazine explicitly states this ('the blue *frames, connects* and *emphasises* the architecture ...' – our italics), which shows that 'grammatical' descriptions are not always written in the register of academic linguistics. This cohesive effect spills over into the adjoining feature advertisement on household goods: crockery, soft furnishings, glassware, napery, etc.: 'Du bleu, du blanc, des rayures, des motifs naifs: ils mettent en beauté, l'été, les objets de tous les jours' ('Blue and white, stripes, simple motifs: they beautify the summer and everyday objects').

Colour clearly functions as a formal semiotic device to provide cohesion and coherence; and this function is active across quite large spans, what in (functional) linguistics is called *colligation.* To test for either, all one needs to do is to take a page from the English magazine, by contrast, and to interleave it with the pages of the French magazine. The entirely differing rules are immediately apparent: the one does not fit with the other; interleaving produces an 'ungrammatical' structure. The precision and the clarity of the rule system of each becomes immediately apparent. There is also cohesion *across* modes. We won't focus on this here although both magazines do: the *textures* of fabrics and ceramics; the *shapes* of glasses, bowls, jugs; the patterns and designs on chair covers, towels, serviettes, plates; the materiality of rock, timber, cement, earthenware, etc. All these are cohesive and provide coherence. In the French magazine the *bleu* and the *blanc* cohere with natural rock, timber, grasses. In the English magazine the oranges and greens cohere with the checks of tablecloths and curtains, and with the turned legs of tables and chairs.

But for colour to be fully a mode, it has to be a resource for making signs: that is, it has to be the signifier-material (the 'stuff', the material, the form) which can be used to carry the signifieds (the 'meanings') of sign-makers. Are colours here used as signs? The choice of colours as signifiers occurs within already established, existent, and well-understood discourses. Colour as signifier is drawn into these discourses, in this case discourses around lifestyle: 'Ce bleu essential donne le tempo et, la maison ayant changé des mains, ses nouveaux propriétaires se sont laissé subjuger comme les précédents' ('This essential blue provides the tempo, and, after the house recently changed hands, the new owners have allowed themselves to be subjected to this like the previous ones'). The point however is that it is not discourse through language which provides the meaning, or shapes these signs, but that the discourse is directly realised in colour (as it is in writing or speech or in other modes).

To side-track for just a moment. For us this is a crucial point, because it promises the key to unlock the barriers to an understanding of colour. That key has so far eluded all those who sought to find it. To put it in our terms, we do not treat colour as sign. We do not say '*Bleu* means *serein*' or '*bleu* means *dure*', or 'green is the colour of hope'. Rather we see colour as a signifier (in the way in which we see all semiotic resources as signifiers at the point of sign-making), which is drawn into sign-making, and is given its signified by the maker of the sign in the context of specific discourses in which and through which the sign-making happens. This means that, as with all signifiers, the signifier material neither fully specifies what the signs which are made can be or will be (e.g. 'green means hope'), nor means that the potentials of the signifier material are completely open ('pink can mean anything you want it to mean, there are no rules'). Rather, a specific colour, as signifier, has, first of all, of itself, a potential for meaning as a signifier due to and in its materiality and interaction with the physiology of bodies. Second, it also has meaning potential because of its cultural history. How that potential will be realised in an actual sign is a matter, jointly, of the interests of the maker of the sign, of the potentials of the signifier material, of the cultural history of that colour (e.g. what specific colours have been given what meanings in what contexts in a given culture, e.g. 'pink is for girls'), and of the discourses within which the sign is articulated. So in the house with the 'minimalist heritage' of *Maison Française* there is a pink table: 'à l'acier... et [à] la table signée Bernard Venet répondent les rayures rouges et marines des toiles de Buren et le rose d'une table-sablier en plexiglas d'Yves Klein' ('to the steel ... and the Bernard Venet table correspond the red and blue stripes of the Buren fabric and the pink sand of the Yves Klein plexiglas coffee table'). In this 'geometrically minimalist' house, pink is clearly not the pink of thousands of congratulations cards welcoming the birth of a baby girl in Anglophone societies. Its use in an architectural and lifestyle discourse, an aesthetic discourse of minimalism 'qui ordonne et rythme l'espace', makes this pink into a quite different sign.

This is, for us, the key: colours are not signs (the common-sense and mistaken assumption of art history and psychology alike); colours are signifiers. As such they become signs – enter into meaning – in the same way as other signifier material does. Where colour is drawn into design, as mode, it is brought in in the manner we have just described: the discourses which exist in the domain of the specific design practice shape the meaning of the colour sign.

In concluding our discussion of the question of colour as mode, we can say that colour is a semiotic mode, and certainly so in specific domains of practice. It is thus one of the 'available resources' for design, sufficiently articulated as a mode, and able to be integrated into the discourses of the domain of practice.

In our next example, the Annapelle card, colour-as-available-resource is again an issue. However, with this example we wish to discuss the matter of 'grammar and design' more directly: the 'grammars' of the resources – the modes – deployed in a design, as much as the 'grammars', the organisation, the shapes, the discourses, which emerge in and which have a shaping effect on design.

The Annapelle card is the size of a credit card; it is made of firm olive-eucalyptus green paper card with a smooth glossy surface; and it has printed language on one side. It came, as one of three identical cards, stuck in a small leather purse, sent as a present from Australia to London in 1996. The modes involved in its design are, clearly, language-as-writing and colour. A question arises whether the card as 'card' has modal aspects – it has a cultural history, and it is related to other cards, to business cards, calling cards, loyalty cards, credit cards, membership cards, etc. The question 'Is this a grammatical (conventional) use of the card?' or 'Is this a membership (or 'business', or 'loyalty') card?' certainly could arise. Is the card-qua-card to be treated as an element of a mode? Our own response would be, as with the term mode (or grammar, or genre, or script), that it depends on the domain of practice, that is, on the precise cultural, social, economic location, and on the occasions in which it is used. Here, in this instance, it may be; in other domains it need not be. Is photography (rather than visual image as such) a mode? If you are a photographer, no doubt our tests would be answered positively; if you are the man or woman in the street, there may, in your practice, not be a modal/grammatical distinction between images in printing, etching, drawing, photography, etc. That is not to say, of course, that the ordinary person in everyday situations is not entirely aware of differences; it is to say that for her or him they do not have modal import.

Similarly with layout: layout is a noticeable feature on this card, so is layout a mode? For the practitioner of magazine, newspaper or textbook production it undoubtedly is: forms of layout are distinctive, regular practices, with regular effects, 'looks' and structures. The question becomes somewhat more difficult when we move to the materiality of the kind of card paper: the thickness of the 'card' as material, its degree of gloss. No doubt for paper manufacturers, as for designers with paper, there are established regularities. Were these known, understood, *available* to the designer?

For us these are questions of absolute significance. 'Our', the 'Western', recent history has left 'us', in the West, with views in which a representational resource (not the term used in that history – the term is our attempt, borrowing from the work of Michael Halliday, precisely to get away from the terminologies of that past with their baggage) either is or is not grammatical, subject to the rigidities, certainties and conventions which are caught up in the term 'grammar'. We think that that is no longer a tenable approach: in some domains a resource is treated as though it were subject to grammar; in others it is not. These boundaries shift over time, and they vary between social-cultural groups. And that which is seen as subject to grammar is constantly subject to the socially contingent transformative action of those who avail themselves of the resource. For us this is not an abandonment of the view that there are regularities (a radical postmodern view) but an assertion that to see representational resources (all the resources available for meaning-making) as subject to and part of social forces is to accept precisely this position.

In the case of the card, the available resources as modes are likely to be writing, layout, colour, card (as cultural/social object), card paper (as material stuff), perhaps in this order of decreasing modal articulation, along a range: writing, certainly, in all domains; card (as material stuff) barely, and only in bounded domains. But these modes were all available to the designer, and were, we believe, made use of by her or him in this instance.

The card is designed for an economic purpose. Reading its texts reveals what that might be. What is this card meant to achieve? Clearly, somehow, it is to add value,

Figure 3.4 *The Annapelle card*

'appeal', to the purse. The text makes it obvious that, apart from the card itself as object, the appeal lies, or is meant to lie, in making it clear that this purse is, despite the histories of its production (made *in* Italian leather, *manufactured* in China), an 'Australian' product. And as an Australian product it is more valuable to Australian consumers than it would be without that quality. To produce this effect, the designers do semiotic work. They draw on a number of discourses: of *nationalism* (the emphasis on Australianness; on Australian ownership; on Australian value and practices); of (mildly expressed) *racism* and *ethnic difference* (the nervousness about standards of manufacture in China, and by contrast the positive evaluation of European manufacture and Australian quality control); of *aesthetics/taste* (the evaluative adjective 'fine'; the term 'handcrafted'); of *economics* and *business* (the use of the jargon of contemporary practices, such as 'quality inspection', and the format of the 'business card'); and *heritage* (the invocation of Europe in the form of Italianness).

Each of these discourses represents organisations of knowledge, values and taste, and each therefore provides a kind of template into which that which is to be designed can be fitted. The ensemble of all these discourses together has to be designed so that at the very least a semblance of coherence exists in the material (textual) object which is its realisation. Together the design of this discursive ensemble has a shaping effect on the modal elements which are used to realise it. To put this simply, the various discourses are expressed (each differently) in a number of modes. For instance, the discourse of nationalism is expressed in writing and colour.

The discourse of aesthetics is realised in colour, layout, writing. The demand to produce a coherent discursive ensemble has a shaping effect on how the modal resources are used. This applies to language-as-writing, but it applies equally to colour, as it does to the other modes.

Designing is active, agentive, yet also hedged by rules, constraints, conventionalised practices on two sides. On the side of resources for design, the modes have cultural articulation through their histories of social use, and these articulations mean that the elements of the modes, and the combinations in which they appear, have a (relative) stability. Design has to work with and against that stability. On the side of that which provides available shapings for the design, the discourses (as well as the scripts and the genres), there are shapings which provide the frames; that which is to be designed has to negotiate with these – broadly these are the frames within which the to-be-designed has to be accommodated.

Here we briefly illustrate what we mean. Take the shaping effect of discourse on the one hand (let us say, the aesthetic discourse) and the constraints of the mode of writing, the *grammar of writing*, on the other hand. The aesthetic discourse emerges, as we said, in the selection of the adjectives 'fine' and 'handcrafted'; but it emerges also in the use of the grammar of this mode. Consider two instances: the use of the relative clause 'which is made in Italian leather' and the use of the preposition 'in' in that clause. This relative clause would normally be a non-restrictive clause; here it is treated as a restrictive relative clause (the distinction between 'a star, which, on a good night, is easily visible' and 'the star which outshines every other near sunset'). The latter makes the object named by the head noun unique, the former does not. 'Uniqueness' is here a sign produced with the resources of the grammar in order to play a part in realising the aesthetic discourse; but it happens somewhat against the grain of normal grammatical usage. That is, this is precisely an instance when in the process of design the constraints are worked against as a result of the demands of the discourse.

A very similar effect is produced, we feel, by the use of the preposition 'in'. This, we feel, would normally be – ought normally to be – the preposition 'of' ('made of Italian leather'), or perhaps 'from' ('made from Italian leather'). 'In' gives a quite special feel, perhaps derived from its qualities as 'container metaphor', to use the Lakoff/Johnson parlance. We are, precisely, 'in' a world of craft, of quality, of tradition, of leather as aesthetic material. And 'in' is also connected to the world of art, in which a sculptor can be said to work 'in bronze' or 'in wood'. Both in the case of the relative clause and in the case of the preposition, grammar, as one aspect of mode, is drawn on as part of the realisational resources for this discourse.

Similarly with punctuation. A linguist's pedantic urge might be to punctuate this brief passage 'properly', with a comma after *company, produce, leather, China,* leaving the other two commas where they are. Again, we feel that the exceedingly sparse punctuation (including the omission of the possessive apostrophe in *People's*) is there as an effect of a design decision: the 'proper' punctuation would make the text look fussy, fiddly. As it is the text looks clean, clear. Punctuation is used as a mode to play its part in the realisation of the aesthetic discourse.

To conclude this discussion, a word or two on the use of colour in this object. One of the discourses at work here is, as we said, that of nationalism. The eucalypt-green colour of the card may therefore be one of the expressions of that discourse in this small text. A different choice might have been made: Australianness could also have been signalled using the red, black and gold colours of the Australian Aboriginal flag. Of course, that choice would have foregrounded the highly political character of choosing colour (another sign of its function as mode): this is decidedly not the Australianness which these designers wished to evoke. Their Australianness is the green of the bush – the colour of 'natural' Australia, standing for an equally specific politics (the ostensive avoidance of the political, but also the politics of Australian environmentalism). But this green can also be read as olive green, and it then 'goes with' the Italianness of the leather, the style of the text, its layout. In other words, colours can have several distinct readings and functions, including, here too, the function of realising the discourse of aesthetics. Lexis, colour, grammar, punctuation, layout, logo, paper are all drawn into the realisation of this discourse. Or, to see it from the point of view of the designer, this discourse (once the design decision has been made to use it) provides a powerful constraining and shaping effect. On the one hand are the available resources, with their 'resistances', on the other hand stand the discourses, offering to shape design decisions in any number of modes. In the centre stands the designer: free yet not free; constrained and hemmed in; and yet creative and transformative. The elements and rules of the semiotic modes have shape and are resistant to a greater or lesser degree to the shaping of the designer; the discourses (and scripts and genres) strongly press in on possible design decisions and suggest how the modes are to be used in actual new designs. The designer works in this confined 'space' – creatively, agentively, transformatively.

Designing as transformation: the shaping of modes and discourse

The purposive process of design works with and on available resources and does so in the environment of the more or less strongly enforced and felt already existing shaping of discourses. In a sense this process might be simply reproductive: the modes are already shaped, and that shape imposes its constraints as well as its affordances on specific discourses and designs. This is perhaps one restatement of what has, in the period of structuralism, been the accepted common sense of representation and communication. Design, however, takes place in the field of social action, and with the agentive force of individual (even if socially/historically shaped) interests. The response to the demands of a new situation requires design decisions which are always significantly different from those taken before. The specific discourses with which a design will be realised will very likely be different from one time to another. New ensembles of discourses ensure that the resultant material semiotic object, whether 'textual' or other, is always new in some significant respect. The appearance of the discursive ensemble and its materialisation as text or other object has its effect on each of the co-present discourses. In the compromise of accommodation to each of the co-present discourses, each discourse is transformed.

There is, equally, transformation of discourse in relation to the modes used: the design process in the multimodal world involves selection of discourses and selection of modes through which content-in-discourse will be realised. To use the mode of image to represent certain information means that the mode of writing is not used for that purpose. That will have an effect on the (elements of the) mode writing. Writing will come to be used for specific purposes, and that shift in use will have its inevitable effects on the shape of signs made in that mode, and therefore on the signifier material. In work we have done elsewhere (Kress and van Leeuwen, 1996) it is clear that the uses of writing in textbooks have undergone a remarkable shift. Where thirty, forty or fifty years ago writing 'carried' all the informational load, with consequent effects on forms of syntax (sentence complexity, forms and frequencies of nominalisation, etc.), in contemporary textbooks there is *functional specialisation.* Language-as-writing is now used to describe (pedagogically salient) actions, events, in quasi-narrative form; image is used to describe the 'shape' of phenomena (circuits, magnetic fields, digestive mechanisms, the carbon cycle) which are the stuff of curricular content.

The design process reshapes, transforms, both writing and image, both as realisational material and as discourses (as well as scripts and genre), and as existent potential shapings.

We will conclude this section with a brief discussion of another example. It may be that the issue of the constant transformation of modal resources in design is uncontentious when it is applied to modes such as writing, speech, image, gesture, etc. We wish to assert that it applies to all cultural objects, and so return once more to that seemingly implausible subject, the house.

The ordinary, common, late nineteenth-century terrace house was built, let us say in 1888, in Sydney or London, to a broadly common design. Despite this common design it had vast variations of overall size, sizes of rooms, and smaller details in the dispositions of rooms, etc.; not to mention the addition of verandas in Australia, the effect there both of climate and a mixture of Indian colonial and Italianate discourses. But such a house, once built, is surely beyond transformation? Yet, as we mentioned in the previous chapter, houses of this kind have been subject to constant transformation. In the 1950s and 1960s bathrooms and indoor toilets were added, and in the 1970s and through the 1980s the dividing walls between the front room and the back room were knocked out, and scullery, kitchen, and outhouse were unified into a single space, while the insertion of glass doors at the back of the house permitted vision and movement into the garden, 'let light into the house', and so on.

These changes were not accidental, they were not arbitrary, nor were they 'individual', even though each individual imagined that she or he was doing this redesign as the expression of individual taste. The changes reflected changed notions of the family, of divisions of public and private – in Australia as in England. They involved a migration from the front of the house to the back, away from the public street to the private garden. They both reflected and produced changing lifestyles, in which, perhaps, a changing climate played its part. They were founded not so much on more leisure as on changed discourses of leisure. And they reflected, precisely, the importation of new discourses of aesthetics, for instance inspired by holidays taken around the Mediterranean.

But, it might be said, these changes happen so infrequently, they are hardly constant transformations. Consider then the minor, the lesser transformations, the decision as to which room will be the parents' bedroom, upstairs at the front of the house or at the back, and which will be the children's rooms, of whether there will be a dining room or just an eating corner in the kitchen, etc. Choices of colours for different rooms are also transformations, related, engendered by discourses of lifestyle, which, in their turn, relate to discourses of the family, of the economy, of work and of leisure. The decision to have the evening meal in the eating corner, with or without the tablecloth, is another transformation, as is the decision to have Sunday lunch in the dining room. Each use of space of the house is transformative – of course made in the light of discourses, as we said in the previous chapter, of family, of work, of leisure, of aesthetics. And the home magazines and television programmes are there to supply, incessantly, designs for this process. These designs are not prescriptive in any strict sense, but they are nevertheless presented as taken up or endorsed by television personalities and other celebrities, and by various kinds of 'model' families, and they come with all the authority of the designers who are constantly presented to the public as the ultimate arbiters of good taste.

4 Production

Production and interpretation

Production is the communicative use of *media*, of *material* resources. The idea of 'medium' includes the body and the voice, and the tools which may extend bodily communication and expression (for instance musical instruments; or the skirts and shoes and castanets in a dance like the flamenco), as well as the tools and materials used in producing artefacts (pen and paper, paint and canvas, chisel and wood, etc.). Our key point will be that production plays an independently variable semiotic role in communication and does not 'merely' realise what we have called 'designs'. Even when a voice reads out what has already been designed as writing, or sings what has already been designed as a musical composition, the speaker or singer's bodily articulation also communicates *directly*, adding meanings which are not pre-figured by the designs. These kinds of meaning are often difficult to describe in words (if they could be described in words they would perhaps no longer communicate directly). They are nevertheless perceived distinctly, and responded to both cognitively and affectively.

Production is always physical work, whether by humans or machines, a physical job of articulating 'text'. And the interpretation of production is also physical work, a use of the body (the sensory organs). Production media are closely associated with different sensory channels, because each medium is characterised by a particular configuration of material qualities, and each of these material qualities is grasped by a particular set of sensory organs. Some can only be grasped perceptively, for instance colour or smell. Others can only be grasped by touch, by handling the object, for instance weight or softness. Again others can be grasped by both, for instance texture – whether something is rough or smooth can not only be felt with the hand or the mouth, but also seen, at least under suitable conditions of illumination, and heard, because we know from experience what happens to the timbre of our voice when our throat is rough and swollen, and we can recognise the resulting hoarse and gravelly quality in other people's voices, as in instrumental timbres. As a result, production can also set up *correspondences* between the material qualities perceived by different sense organs. This in turn explains why so many of the terms that denote material qualities can travel between semiotic modes, why we can have 'loud' colours, 'warm' colours, and 'vowel' colours, 'bright' sounds, 'sharp' sounds and 'dull' sounds, etc., in short why we can have synaesthesia, multimedial meaning, meaning which can be materially realised and recognised in different media.

It follows that multimodality and multimediality are not quite the same thing. Radio (which is of course a distribution medium rather than a production medium) is multimodal in its affordances, because it involves speech, music and other sounds; but it is monomedial, since it can only be heard, and not seen, smelled, touched or tasted. Everyday face to face interaction, on the other hand, is both multimodal (it uses speech, non-verbal communication and so on) and multimedial (it addresses the eye and the ear and potentially also touch, smell and taste). It therefore also follows that, just as a given mode (e.g. language) may be realised in different media (e.g. speech and handwriting), so several modes (e.g. language, pictures) may be realised in the same medium (e.g. painting, or moulded plastic). All this speaks for the relative independence of mode and medium: if the two are coupled, as when production media (e.g. the actor's or singer's voice) are 'slaved' to design modes (e.g. a dramatic or musical script), then this is the result of a particular and quite specific form of the social organisation of semiosis.

Interpreting 'production' is never a matter of passive reception. This is clear, say, in the case of touch. But touch should not be opposed too strongly to the other senses. Touch is also a form of perception, just as looking at things is also, in a sense, touching them, a form of action. It is not the case, as we have stressed in earlier chapters, that seeing and hearing are passive, and that touching is active. In both cases it can either be that a sensation imposes itself on us unbidden, or that we actively scan the environment with our sensory organs; either that we become aware, suddenly or gradually, of a darkening of the visual field, a foul or agreeable smell, a glowing of heat or a cold draught, or that we actively scan the environment with our eyes and our ears, sniff around to find the source of a smell, or explore an object with our hands, all this notwithstanding the fact that social constraints will make us privilege some senses and repress others in most domains, at least once we have outgrown our earliest childhood. Rowan Atkinson has his Mr Bean character walk through a supermarket and try out the merchandise through touch and taste. He picks up a frying pan, takes the wrappings off, digs up a fish which he just happens to have in his inexhaustible clown's trouser pockets, puts the fish in a pan, and then jiggles the pan with an appreciative smile. He takes a toothbrush from the shelves, takes the wrapping off, feels the bristles, and tries it out on his teeth before putting it back again. The comic effect derives of course precisely from the taboo on touch and taste as modes of sensing in public, and it brings home how much the supermarket has become a monomedial (visual) rather than a multimedial experience (although packaging is of course multimodal, involving modes such as words, pictures, typography, layout, three-dimensional form etc.).

At the same time, there is also a difference between, on the one hand, sight and sound and smell, and, on the other hand, touch and taste. With our hands and mouth we can perceive material objects as well as transform them, with or without the aid of instruments. Maybe the same can be said to some extent of the eye. Looks can kill, they say, and looks can also mesmerise a person or animal. But the looks that can kill, the sounds that can alarm, the smells that mark the territory, are interactions with our fellow creatures and not with material objects. Material objects we can see, but not change with our eyes, hear, but not change with our voice, smell, but not change with our chemical excretions. For this we have only two organs, our hands and our mouth. There is therefore a fluid boundary between the production and the active perception of material qualities, and hence also between 'reading texts' and 'using artefacts'. Reading text is also active. It involves active mental work. But that work is taking place on the levels of discourse and design, and it leads, as we said, to 'inward production'. It is mental work. Modern computer interfaces try to make perception and reading more physical. Physical manipulation of objects (the mouse, the joy stick, the pressure pen, the touch screen, etc.) replaces visual scanning. Reading text becomes more like using artefacts, and hence at least potentially also more transformative, always allowing users not only to read but also to rewrite, not only to use but also to adapt. What has long been argued in theory, has already begun to be implemented in practice in computer interfaces.

The key point, however, remains this: meaning does not only reside in discourse and design, it also resides in production. It results from human engagement with the world, and the resources we use in articulating and interpreting meaning comprise both semiotic modes and semiotic media. It is the effect of a particular kind of semiotic/cognitive/affective work: the integration by an individual of a semiotic element (or complex of semiotic elements) into their already existing – and constantly transformed – systems of classification. Such semiotic elements exist in all available semiotic modes and media. It is too obvious to state that we can remember smells and tastes, and that we are able to compare and grade them. If this is so then meaning is made through these media also.

Finally, media are socially formed. This applies to the body and the voice as much as to the materials we use in producing semiotic artefacts. Of course, the fact of their existence can be considered pre-semiotic, and certain of their pre-semiotic characteristics will place constraints on their semiotic potential. But it is really only at the beginning of life that we can see the body in its pre-semiotic form. From then on all the aspects of the body and the voice that matter are socially formed, and those that are not are either hidden or never noticed. We will expand on this later in the chapter when we discuss the speaking and singing voices of men and women. And the same applies to materials. Boards of timber are material for the carpenter and the builder. But they too are already socially formed. One of their qualities may be that they are smooth. But why are they smooth? Not because they grow that way, but because someone has sawn and planed them. And who is that someone? That depends. Whether timber is going to be rough or smooth may be decided at different stages of the production process – by the manufacturer, the distributor or retailer, the end user. The question therefore also becomes the question of who controls this particular aspect of the meaning of wood. The same line of thought can be applied to food, another case which demonstrates the active production of meaning through materiality and the active use of meaning in consumption. Potatoes are a natural product (although perhaps less and less so as genetic engineering intrudes). But they may, for instance, be mashed in a factory and bought from the supermarket shelves in already-mashed form. Or they may be mashed in the kitchen and served up with a sprinkling of parsley. Or I may mash them on my plate, in the gravy. What then is the material quality of potatoes? Are they hard or soft? This is not the right question. The point is rather that material qualities relate to social practices of transforming materials. Material qualities inhere in material substances but they are then transformed: they are socially (re)produced. They too are controlled, in a form of control which is ultimately control over meaning, and over social values – which may rest with the individual or with large and powerful social institutions.

The anthropologist Bronislaw Malinowski (1935: 50) tells how Trobriand Islander children, out in the gardens with their parents, picked up attractive flowers or coloured leaves and showed them to the adults, only to be told: 'Throw it away since it is a weed'. Materials which have not been recognised as materials are disregarded and do not enter the realm of meaning. And yet, one day their material qualities may suddenly suggest a semiotic potential. Thus the material world is always in part already medium, in part as yet only potential medium.

Production as the realisation of design

Linguists and semioticians have generally regarded 'production' as the realisation of design, and hence as not adding any further meaning, or as adding, at best, only a layer of expressiveness, of 'bringing the design to life'. This engendered a semiotics in which matter did not matter. It produced a linguistics which treated the handwritten and the printed sentence, the sentence written in the sand and the sentence carved in stone, as identical for the purposes of linguistic analysis. This was a semiotics which could apply the same analysis to a painting, an etching, a relief sculpture, a photograph, and disregard their material differences; a semiotics which treated matter as distinct from meaning, as the business of physicists, phoneticians and forensic scientists, or, in the case of art, of the experts who assess the age and authenticity of art works. But the same design with a different material production does not mean quite the same thing. Signs in neon light do not mean the same thing as hand-painted signs on a wooden board, nor do documents on heavy embossed paper mean the same thing as documents on grey recycled paper.

In disregarding matter in this way, linguists and semioticians followed a cultural trend in which the de-contextualised power of design reigned over the specificities, the practicalities and the realities of everyday life and art, in which, for instance, musical scores or playscripts had come to be regarded as constituting the identity of musical and dramatic works, rather than the sounds and body movements which actually materialise the works, or in which all painters were using the same kinds of canvas and oils, all typewriters the same font, all games and other computer texts the same glass screen, so that materiality as a source of difference, and hence of meaning, had become marginalised or sidetracked. But the semiotic potential of production is difficult to repress and much theoretical effort was devoted to trying to contain it – in trying to prove, for instance, that intonational phrasing follows and simply 'marks' grammatical clauses (Crystal, 1975), with at best an optional emotive 'key' added (Halliday, 1967), or that stress can be predicted lexically, systematically, rather than that it is a more loosely organised way of highlighting important moments, that it operates separately from, yet simultaneous with grammar, and is not only less systematically organised but also multimedial (Van Leeuwen, 1999).

This was not the only way in which the semiotic potential of production has been kept away from view. Production has also often been psychologised. Handwriting, for instance, has been, and still is, seen as a more or less automatic reflex of character, and the social history of regulating handwriting through the education system has generally been kept out of the interpretation of handwriting. Non-verbal communication ('body language') has also been psychologised, and is commonly seen as symptomatic of affective processes such as nervousness, boredom, sexual attraction, etc., rather than as semiotic action people consciously engage in (or at any rate at least as consciously as they engage in speech). Writers like Desmond Morris (1977) manage to combine the ethological ('naked ape') approach to body language with observations of the many cultural differences between simple gestures such as 'yes' and 'no' gestures, etc., without addressing the contradiction this involves.

The post-structuralist emphasis on the 'pleasure of the text' can also side-track the semiotic potential of production. Julia Kristeva, for instance, opposed the semiotic mode (as we would call it) of language to the medium of speech. The medium of speech, she argued, adds rhythm, and rhythm is on the side of desire and pleasure, while the mode of language is on the side of obeying the codes and laws of society (Kristeva, 1980: 159–209). Roland Barthes, in 'The Grain of the Voice' (1977: 179–89), opposed 'the features which belong to the structure of the language being sung, the rules of the genre, the coded form of the composer's idiolect, the style of the interpretation: in short everything in the performance which is in the service of communication, representation, expression' to 'the grain of the voice', 'the materiality of the body speaking its mother tongue', 'something which is directly brought to your ears in one and the same movement from deep down in the cavities, the muscles, the membranes, the cartilages'. The 'grain of the voice', he said, affects the listener in a completely personal, even quasi-erotic way, providing pleasure and escaping the semiotic and the social. Perhaps this view only reversed the polarities, placing on a pedestal what before was marginalised as 'mere performance', and keeping semiotics, and hence (socially produced) meaning, firmly restricted to what we have called 'design'. Of course it also opposed pleasure and meaning, suggesting that pleasure is somehow a realm apart, wholly individual and a-social. In our view pleasures (or un-pleasures) are always (though not always to the same extent) attached to meanings, and a vital aspect of communication. Communication never just 'communicates', 'represents' and 'expresses', it also always and at the same time affects us. The two cannot be separated. Even when communication seeks to do the opposite, the very fact of negating materiality affects us – by failing to engage us affectively.

Meaning can also be replaced with economic value, or with taste or fashion value. The former often happens in relation to film and theatre, where the production of a play or the adaptation or a novel can be 'simple' and 'sober' or 'lavish' and high in 'production value'. The latter is typically used in relation to the consumer goods with which we express our identity, to furniture, food, dress and so on. These are held to be a matter of taste, and taste is held to be individual rather than social, hence not semiotic. That taste is not entirely individual has been well established in sociology (e.g. Bourdieu, 1986), although sociological accounts do not always recognise that personal identification with a shared, social taste is not a passive process of conforming to a norm but as active a process as learning to express yourself in a new language. From this perspective meaning and taste are not so different. To speak of 'meaning' is to recognise openly that something is shared; to speak of 'taste' is to negate this. At the same time, 'meaning' has often been used in the sense of normative, 'fixed' meaning, rather than in the sense of a 'reading' which (depending on the context) may be quite personal, even if it is constructed out of resources that are made available socially; and 'meaning' has also often been seen as cognitive/rational, and not as (also) involving affect. 'Taste' brings out some elements of contemporary semiosis which traditionally have been neglected in semiotics and, in the matter of production, we could therefore do with some kind of synthesis of 'meaning' and 'taste' (see Kress, 1998).

The term 'fashion' differs from 'taste' in that it openly includes the idea of conforming. But it is similar in that it does not include the idea of meaning. In his work on fashion, Barthes (1967) made meaning and fashion value two distinct levels of meaning, on the ground that both are explicitly stated in the texts which accompany the pictures in fashion magazines. Thus a caption like 'these fresh new cottons preview a delicious turn towards very feminine fashion' (Van Leeuwen, 1983: 23) makes the meaning of a fabric, hence a medium (cottons) explicit as 'fresh' and 'feminine'. It also makes the fashion value of cottons explicit: 'new', 'preview trend towards fashion'. Barthes's book includes some excellent pages on material qualities such as 'heavy' and 'light', but on the whole he concentrates on the text of fashion magazines, an institution which seeks to influence people's interpretations, rather than on the garments themselves, and on people's own interpretations of fashion meanings, their choices of what to wear and of how to wear it, and their ideas about why they wear what they wear.

The semiotics of production: provenance

Explanations of Roland Barthes's concepts of 'myth' and 'connotation' usually centre either on his formal, Hjelmslevian definition of 'connotation', or on the ideological nature of the signified which is expressed by the term 'myth'. As Barthes initially formulated them, 'myth' and 'connotation' are 'parasitical' signs, signs which use an already formulated 'literal' or 'denotative' sign and load it with a secondary or connotative meaning which then pushes the literal, denotative meaning into the background, as it were. This secondary meaning, covering the real with a layer of 'myth', is ideological. Thus a picture of a saluting black soldier in French uniform (in the 1950s) can come to express the ideology of (French) imperialism. Later Barthes modified the idea that there could be an ideologically innocent primary meaning and called, not just for 'the destruction of the (ideological) signified', or 'mythoclasm', but also for 'the destruction of the sign', or 'semioclasm' (1977: 167). In our terms, he became interested, not just in discourse, but also in design and production, in the semiotic modes and media themselves.

Two other, perhaps less often foregrounded aspects of Barthes's concepts of 'connotation' and 'myth' have helped us generate our notion of 'provenance'. The first is that 'mythical' signifieds are 'imported' from some other domain (some other place, time, social group, culture) to signify a complex of ideas and values which are associated with that 'other' domain by those who do the importing. Barthes's example in 'Rhetoric of the Image' (1977: 32–51) is an advertisement for Panzani pasta, sauce and parmesan. The name Panzani and the colour scheme of the advertisement (based on the Italian flag) signify, not 'Italy', but 'Italianicity', a 'specifically "French" knowledge' of things associated with Italy: 'an Italian would barely perceive the connotation of the name, no more probably than he would the Italianicity of tomato and pepper' (1977: 34). Again, in *Mythologies*, Barthes had used '*sinité*' ('Chinese-ness') as an example, 'a certain mélange of bells, rikshas and opium dens' (1972: 121). John Berger, in discussing advertising images, also hints at the idea of importing signifiers from different times and places when he says that 'myths' use history and geography to lend meaning to advertised products so that 'cigars can be sold in the name of a King, underwear in connection with the Sphinx, a new car by reference to the status of a country house'. These references 'are imprecise and ultimately meaningless ...: they should not be understandable, they should merely be reminiscent of cultural lessons half-learnt' (1972: 140).

This brings us to the second point, the 'imprecision' of the meanings that are conveyed in this way. 'Mythical' signifiers signify whole discourses, in the sense in which we have used the term in this book: a version of events (e.g. what Italians or Chinese or Kings do) together with the (positive or negative) values and ideas attached to this. But these discourses are never explicitly formulated. They are only evoked. The implication is that people already know them. People think they know what is meant, despite the vagueness, and despite the fact that they would probably not be able to put that knowledge into words. As a result no questions are asked. And what is more, 'myth' is never neutral, but is always invested with affect, with a strong sense of positive or negative evaluation.

Although provenance may involve semiotic modes from the 'places' where the signifiers come from, from the point of view of the 'place' that *imports* the signifier there is no connection with design. Production and discourse are directly connected. There is no 'code', no system, merely a loose collection of historical and geographical references. The discourse itself is therefore not the object of systematic and explicit knowledge. It is merely hinted at, merely evoked. This does not mean that it is unimportant. Moral discourses are, for many people in the West, no longer systematically and explicitly known. They have gone underground. Most of us have only a few key words, a few icons, a few exemplary stories, to hint at the submerged and no longer explicitly known, but still powerful systems of Christian morality, and their philosophical offshoots. Something similar applies to new languages such as that of computer icons. There is as yet only an unstructured collection of individual icons. We must either grasp the intertextualities and metaphors or remember the meaning of every icon separately. There is not as yet a system or a language to help us.

Our notion of provenance, then, includes these aspects:

1. In the absence of a semiotic mode, that is, of an explicitly worked out 'lexicogrammar', one mode of signifying a discourse is through provenance, through attaching a discourse to a signifier imported from another place, another time, another culture, or another social group, where this other 'place' is, in one way or another, related to or associated with key values or themes from that discourse.
2. A sign that signifies through provenance evokes a complete discourse, but without making that discourse explicit, so that, subjectively, only a vague and confused complex of ideas and values is communicated. Nevertheless, these ideas and values are usually important to the 'place' which has created the provenance sign, and they are associated with strong feelings. As a result the vagueness is not usually consciously realised.
3. Communication by means of provenance is usually unsystematic and *ad hoc*, an invention of the moment, or part of a catalogue of past inventions which has never been systematised, and can therefore only be communicated as a 'list'. In

the same way there will be no general rules for interpretation, so that each case is seen as unique, and examples can only be interpreted one at a time.

Here are some examples. Travelling with a particular airline, we were surprised to see that the cabin crew wore obligatory blue jeans with their (strictly identical) uniforms, which, for the rest, included items we would normally consider typical of air crew uniforms, such as red waistcoats, white shirts and blouses, scarves, ties. Wearing blue jeans in the workplace usually means that one is free to choose what to wear (the fact that so many people make the identical choice is not the issue here). For those who may not wear blue jeans at work, they are associated with leisure, with private time. The cabin crew uniforms, however, introduced blue jeans as part of an obligatory uniform and so combined connotations of leisure (the 'provenance' of blue jeans) and connotations of work, thus allowing employees to wear, and passengers to see, the new discourse of 'flexitime' work practices which increasingly diminish the boundaries between 'the time of the boss' and 'your own time', without perhaps even being aware of what it is they wear and see. This new use of blue jeans is of course not the only migration in the history of blue jeans as they moved up the social ladder from their origins as a cheap work outfit for American dock workers.

The same can apply to the material or 'non-distinctive' qualities of sound. In French music of the late eighteenth century, hurdy-gurdies were introduced into the orchestra, because these instruments were used in the folk music of the country, and their timbre connoted the values of unspoilt rural life which played such a role in the dominant culture of the period (these were of course not the values of the country people themselves). The hurdy-gurdy eventually didn't make it in the orchestra, but the drone persisted as a key feature of pastoral themes (Winternitz, 1979). Or, take an example related to speech rather than music: in Holland, in the 1960s, it was fashionable for left-wing intellectuals and artists to mix a bit of broad Amsterdam accent in their speech, whether or not they hailed from that city. Amsterdam was then the 'red' city, the centre of the cultural and political experiments of the period. In the 1980s, however, many 'progressive' artists and intellectuals managed to acquire just a little tinge of broad Rotterdam accent – and Rotterdam's image as a centre of commerce and enterprise was a different one, suitable to the age of the 'yuppie'.

The semiotics of production: experiential meaning potential

Material qualities can also acquire meaning, not on the basis of 'where they come from', but on the basis of our physical, bodily experience of them. But what do these qualities mean? They mean in the first place what they are. 'Soft' means 'soft', and 'hard' means 'hard'. But, as Lakoff and Johnson (1980) and Lakoff (1987) have shown, extensive metaphorical edifices can be derived from this. One of the examples they use is 'brittleness' (1980: 28):

> When a brittle object shatters, its pieces go flying, with possibly dangerous consequences. Thus, for example, when someone goes crazy and becomes wild or violent, it would be appropriate to say 'He broke down'. Ontological metaphors like these are so natural and pervasive in our thought that they are usually taken as self-evident, direct descriptions of mental phenomena ... Metaphors like THE MIND IS A BRITTLE OBJECT are an integral part of the model of the mind that we have in this culture.

According to Lakoff, our early experience of moving our bodies in space and of interacting with the material world forms the basis of our ability to develop abstract concepts through metaphor. This view of cognition is neither 'objectivist', because it does not assume the existence of facts independent of belief, knowledge, perception (1987: 164), nor 'subjectivist', because it posits a common, shared basis for human cognition. In our terms this means that humans have the ability to match concepts with appropriate material signifiers on the basis of their physical experience of the relevant materials.

To take an example, softness is a material quality that comes into being for us when we touch creatures or things. By extension, it can then also become a quality of sounds, of colours and so on. From the experience of softness a wide field of potential meanings and cultural values can be derived, to be narrowed down by the specific contexts in which softness is used as a signifier. Softness can mean 'comfort' and 'sensuality' and 'gentleness', but also 'yielding-ness', 'weakness', 'lack of discipline' and 'indulgence', and which precise meanings will prevail and how they are valued depends on who or what is soft, even if these more precise meanings will at the same time also retain their associations with the whole field. Thus it can be that in a given period 'WOMEN ARE SOFT', and that it is, in that period (say North America in the 1950s), 'good' for women to be soft (although they had to become somewhat less soft during the Second World War, when they were needed in the workforce, as can be seen, for instance, in the film *Rosie the Riveter*). Hence women will have to have soft hair, wear soft clothes in soft pastel colours, not have hard muscles, speak softly, eat soft cakes, and so on. At the same time the dominant value of the culture may be hardness, so that softness is highly valued for women, but not highly valued in the culture as a whole, with the result that *women* are not highly valued. All the meanings of 'soft' resonate here in a complex whole: 'comfortable' and 'sensual' as well as 'lacking rigour, strength and discipline'. In the 1960s a number of different vanguards of North American culture attempted to change this, and to make 'soft' a dominant value. Hippies wore soft clothes. Designers introduced soft chairs. Claes Oldenburgh began to make his soft sculptures. But it didn't last: to be a 'softie' or 'a soft touch' is still no praise.

Many material qualities apply, not only to material objects, but also to the movements of the body, and the sound of the voice – by extension we can then project them into other movements and other sounds. A rough voice, for instance, is one in which we can hear other things besides the tone of the voice itself – friction, hoarseness, harshness, rasp. The opposite of the rough sound is the clean, smooth, well-oiled sound from which all noisiness is eliminated. Again, the meaning of roughness lies in what it is: rough. The rough voice (think of Louis Armstrong) is the vocal equivalent of the weather-beaten face, the roughly plastered wall, the faded jeans, the battered leather jacket. The smooth voice is the equivalent of the unblemished young skin, the polished surface, designer plastic, the immaculate tuxedo. How this is valued depends on the context. In western classical music perfection and polish are highly valued. In the Afro-American tradition, on the other hand, roughness is highly valued:

> In most traditional singing there is no apparent striving for the 'smooth' and 'sweet' qualities that are so highly regarded in the Western tradition. Some outstanding blues, gospel and jazz singers have voices that may be described as foggy, hoarse, rough or sandy. Not only is this kind of voice not derogated, it often seems to be valued. Sermons preached in this type of voice appear to create a special emotional tension. (Courlander, quoted in Williams-Jones, 1975: 377)

This can even apply to the basic materials of speech, the vowels and consonants. What is their semiotic value? For most twentieth-century linguists the answer has been: none. 'Phonemes', speech sounds, have no intrinsic, but only distinctive value. They only serve to tell words apart from each other – if a language has both a [p] and a [b], then the different qualities of these consonants serve to tell apart words like [pet] and [bet] or [pail] and [bail], which would otherwise sound identical. An analogous theory of colour would treat colour as serving only to distinguish objects from each other, not to depict the colours of the world, nor to create emotive impact. Poets on the other hand have always known that speech sounds have their own, special meanings. Rimbaud proclaimed:

> I have invented the colour of the vowels! – A black, E white, I red, O blue, U green – I have ordered the form and the movement of each consonant, and with instinctive rhythms I have flattered myself that I have invented a poetic verb, accessible one day or another to every sense. (1960: 228)

In interpreting the sounds of speech on the basis of their experiential meaning potential, a few things have to be remembered. First, every sound is a bundle of different qualities. The [ɪ] (as in [bit]) is not only 'little' (because of leaving a small cavity in the mouth, of being a 'closed' vowel), it is also frontal, requiring the tongue to move towards the front of the mouth, and 'high', requiring the tongue to move up. Second, speech sounds, as opposed to non-speech vocalisations like *mmmm* or *sssh*, come in syllables, so the word 'big' (which people have used to contradict the idea that words with [ɪ] are always little, as in *little, itty-bitty, piccolo*) also has the [b] and the [g] and it is the combination of these which must be interpreted, just as, in the case of colour, it is the combination of colour qualities (saturation, brightness, modulation etc.) which matters. The word [big] for instance has both the 'combustive' bang of the [b] *and* the frontality of the [ɪ]. In other words, the 'big-ness' of [b] is both 'explosive' and 'up front' – quite different from the 'big-ness' of 'large', which is more distant and slow-moving. Critics who dismiss sound symbolism because not all words with an [ɪ] denote something small assume a 'code book' approach to meaning in which every individual item has a fixed meaning. Some meanings are like this. But others come about on the basis of quite flexible semiotic principles (see on this Hodge and Kress, 1988).

This brings out some further key principles of 'experiential meaning potential'. First, it is particularly suited for the expression of the broad value systems of a culture which are expressed through the material qualities of a whole range of cultural artefacts, from food, through to dress and architecture, and through the whole range of ways in which the members of a culture behave physically. This is not to say of course that experiential meaning potential cannot be used for very local meanings. Epstein's sculpture *Jacob and the Angel* is an enormous and heavy sculpture. Its size helps express the massive force involved in the struggle between Jacob and the Angel. It is also made of alabaster, which is reddish brown and *veined*, and this makes the force of the struggle not so much the blind force of anorganic nature, but the force of life. Second, actual materials always have many more qualities than just one, and so they allow more than one analogy to be developed in semiosis. A given material quality, moreover, can relate to different experiences, as in the case of *soft* which can relate to bad experiences (soft soil, on which it is bad to build) as well as good experiences (soft beds, in which it is good to sleep). Third, experiential meaning potentials are typically multimedial, and at the basis of synaesthetic correspondences. Many things can be 'rough' or 'smooth' – a voice, a piece of furniture, a fabric, etc. – so that 'roughness' and 'smoothness' can become a factor in the unity of a taste or a fashion, and hence in the coding orientation or habitus of a culture or a social group. If you like the voice of Louis Armstrong you will perhaps also like rough timber floorboards and roughly plastered walls. If you like smooth voices, you will probably also like polished furniture and shiny parquet floors. And there are discourses behind such tastes and fashions, discourses about what is natural and unnatural, civilised and uncivilised, and so on.

One further example will serve to bring out how this kind of experiential semiosis can signify discourses. Traditional Jewish upbringing involved giving very young children sweets in the form of Hebrew characters, to make them invest their desire in learning as early as possible. But sweets, and food generally, as a mode of communication, are not restricted to Jewish upbringing. One of the key sweets in the Netherlands is '*drop*', Dutch liquorice. It is universally disliked, except by the Dutch of course. Its key material qualities are: (1) it has the consistency of a toffee, initially hard, then softening somewhat as you chew and suck it – but unlike the toffee it never breaks or softens enough to swallow it prematurely, so that it remains hard work to the end; (2) the juices that are extracted from it with so much effort are not sweet but salty; and (3) it is black. Despite having the consistency and shape of a sweet, and despite occupying the social space of a sweet, Dutch liquorice is black and salted. All these qualities relate to key moral values. The hardness of liquorice teaches delayed gratification, saving, restraint, important virtues in the dominant Dutch tradition that go quite a long way back: seventeenth-century travellers already commented that the Dutch are 'frugal to the saving of an egg-shell' and that their 'parsimonious and thrifty living is so extraordinary that a merchant of one hundred thousand pounds estate will scarce spend as much per annum as one of fifteen hundred pounds estate in London' (quoted in Schama, 1987: 295). As for the salty taste, the salted herring or *pekelharing* has a very important place in Dutch history, and is regarded as 'the patriotic fish, the foundation of the national fortune' (Schama, 1987: 165). It was through learning to preserve herring and building the boats necessary for fishing for it that the Dutch learned the skills which laid the foundations for their later merchant fleet and trade empire. As a result, salted herring was, in Holland, a fit subject for literature, as in Westerbaen's verse eulogy 'Lof des Pekelhareng' (In Praise of Salted Herring). Centuries later the salted herring would still be a symbol of how great things could come out of humble beginnings. Not surprisingly there are more 'salt' metaphors in Dutch than in English, and many of them are variants of one basic metaphor: (DUTCH) CIVILISATION IS SALTED. The Dutch have 'salt in their blood', a strong sense of connection with the sea. When they drop all civility they speak the 'unsalted truth'. When they lack wit, their jokes are 'saltless'. Finally, black and white were the colours which Calvinist Dutch ministers prescribed as one of the key features of the Dutch dress code from the seventeenth century onwards. Sweets are clearly used to discipline oral pleasures towards important cultural values and life goals. The anthropologist Jennifer Biddle tells of the first language lesson of her fieldwork among the Warlpiri in the Northern Territory of Australia (personal communication). Her instructor, an older Warlpiri woman, announced that, for a first lesson, they would go hunting: 'If you want to speak Warlpiri, you must first eat Warlpiri'. In the same way the Dutch too 'eat their culture' – as we now all eat the mythologies of Americanness in McDonalds, of Frenchness in the ubiquitous *croissant*, and so on.

From medium to mode

The principles of provenance and experiential meaning potential are always at work in production, whether production is a layer of meaning added in the process of realising a design, or evokes a discourse directly. They are also the materials of which modes are made. Semiosis begins at the level of production. The principles of semiosis which we have discussed in this chapter are at the origin of all meaning, whether for the child who discovers the world, or for the adult who struggles to express newly emerging feelings, meanings and experiences. When such feelings, meanings and experiences become important enough, society may seek to control and maintain them more closely, and modes will come into being. Content as well as expression will be developed into more abstract, more explicit and more systematic forms of knowledge. In a sense this is also what we do in our own work when we develop more abstract and explicit ways of talking about previously marginalised ways of making meaning, such as sound. It is perhaps not surprising that we should be doing this in a world where, for instance, the formerly merely distinctive 'regulation' colours of trains and buses must now express the identity of companies, and where even the sounds of closing car doors are designed to be meaningful and pleasurable, rather than just a mechanical and meaningless by-product of closing the door. When things of this kind happen, colour and sound acquire much enhanced roles in public communication, and the time will not be far off when they will become subject matter of explicit discourses, for instance in education and training.

Technology plays an increasing role in changing media into modes, and hence in controlling how meanings can be made. Word processors, for instance, must systematise such things as the thickness and positioning of the lines that separate sections of text, and develop a metalanguage, whether visual or verbal, for making these choices explicit. Synthetic materials also partake in this process. We will discuss one of them, plastic, at greater length. Plastic was originally developed as a surrogate for various comparatively rare luxury materials which were in short supply, such as ivory, shellac and mother-of-pearl. As such it was already somewhat abstract: it had some of the qualities of the materials it imitated (those that can be grasped visually) but lacked others (those that can be grasped with the ear, the hand, the mouth). The electronic sounds that imitate non-electronic musical instruments are also abstract in this way – they have the harmonic structure of the instruments they imitate, but lack texture, friction, the sound of breath or of bows, plectrums or fingers on strings.

However, the very qualities which set plastic apart from the materials it imitated could also become signifiers in their own right. Precisely because plastic lacked texture and the signs of wear and tear, precisely because it looked so pure and ageless, it could also come to be seen as an object of wonder, and as the essence of modernity. In the 1930s designer Paul Frankl thought plastic was the dream of alchemists come true: 'it transmutes base materials into marvels of beauty' (quoted in Meikl, 1990: 44). More recently Roland Barthes (1972: 54–5 and 97–8) was in two minds. On the one hand he called plastic 'a miraculous substance' and 'a spectacle to be deciphered' which 'hardly exists as substance', on the other hand he called it 'graceless', and 'destroying all the pleasure, the sweetness, the humanity of touch', while its colours were 'mere names', 'able to display only concepts of colour'. On the level of production, plastic was so unlike other materials that it formed a semiotic mystery. It could be rejected because it lacked some of the most essential qualities of physical materiality, or it could be venerated because of this very 'meta'-physicality. It could be seen as a medium or as a mode, or as something in between.

One reason to see plastic as a mode is that it does not have its own specific material qualities. The many kinds of plastic, as defined in terms of organic chemistry, cannot be matched with kinds of plastic as they might be defined semiotically. Almost every kind of plastic can be made available as sheets, fibres, foams, pellets, etc., and almost every kind of plastic can be made hard or soft, heavy or light, thin or thick, red or green and so on, even though some tend towards some qualities more than others. Plastic is already a 'language', a system to signify material qualities, a material 'that adapts itself to the syntax of the design in the same way that the words of a language adapt themselves to the syntax of a text' (Manzini, 1990: 138). Baudrillard (1996: 112) said something similar earlier: 'The manufacture of synthetics signifies for materials a stepping back from their natural symbolism towards a polymorphism, towards a superior level of abstraction which enables a game of the universal associations to take place'. At present we still lack the words to express what these associations might be and how its syntax might work. But, according to Sylvia Katz, plastics expert at the Victoria and Albert Museum (1990: 150), 'before the century runs out a new lexicon will have to be created for plastic, a terminology that can be understood in a direct, non-technical way'.

As a result, plastic objects do not necessarily have uniform material characteristics. Comparing two plastic dolls, Sindy and Action Man, shows that Action Man's head is harder than that of Sindy. Sindy's head can be squeezed, Action Man's head cannot. Their bodies, on the other hand, are equally hard and shiny, and their heads equally dull. Finally, Action Man's synthetic hair is rougher to the touch than Sindy's. Clearly plastic can be used to articulate differences, and hence meanings – here gender differences and gender meanings. These meanings, moreover, are perceived, not visually, but with the hands, as the dolls are posed or played with.

Some of the material qualities which plastic can express are visual: colour, patterning (plastic can be plain, veined, mottled, and so on), translucency (plastic can be transparent, 'cloudy', translucent, opaque), and reflectancy (plastic can be shiny or dull). Other qualities are tactile: taste, weight, hardness, smoothness, and waxiness, and also kinetic qualities (can it fold, stretch, bend; can it be scratched, torn, snapped, broken, etc.). Again other qualities can be heard (does it squeak, ring, etc.), and different plastics may also smell differently and be more or less warm to the touch. All these qualities can acquire significance on the basis of provenance or experiential meaning potential, which we will try to demonstrate by comparing two plastic toothbrush containers.

The main similarities and differences can be listed as follows:

toothbrush container 1	toothbrush container 2
flesh-coloured	white
plain	plain
slightly translucent	slightly translucent
shiny	shiny
comparatively light	comparatively heavy
slightly bendable	rigid
smooth	smooth with ribbed grooving

Some of the differences between these two objects may be interpreted on the basis of provenance – the colours, for example, are in the one case the colour of flesh, in the other white, which speaks of hospitals, and hence of values such as sterility, hygiene, etc. Others are based on the different feel of the two objects – the one is light, flexible and smooth (also sleeker and more streamlined), the other heavier, and sturdier. The one therefore perhaps speaks of a pleasurable pampering of the body beautiful, the other of values of practicality and durability. This brief example hopefully shows that simple everyday objects, which might be considered purely practical and functional, can nevertheless invoke discourses through the way material qualities are articulated, through their sheer *plasticity.* As Italian historian of technology Manzini (1990: 133) has said: 'Plastics have exploited their formidable qualities not so much in the direction of fulfilling technical and constructional needs as in the expression of different images'.

Voice and gender

In our final example we want to emphasise the materiality of the body by looking at the speaking and singing voice. Voice quality is yet another semiotic resource which has not developed into a mode. Explicit discourses of voice quality were mostly concerned with the 'ideal voice', the voice that 'enunciates clearly' and has 'correct diction', just as classical music developed a single style of voice production at which different singers then excel to different degrees. For the rest, voice quality was seen as biological, an involuntary 'fingerprint' of people's unique identity. Linguists and phoneticians (e.g. Crystal, 1969; Laver, 1980) who describe the physical aspects of voice production in great detail, nevertheless offer only a few casual observations about the meaning of different voice qualities. Meanwhile the voice was of course widely used as a semiotic resource, in everyday conversation, in the theatre, in television commercials, in animation films, in popular music, and so on. But even there no systematic approach developed. A handbook for puppeteers (Meilink, 1953: 36) contains a veritable lexicon of gestures ('surprise: raise the head and hands', 'anger: bend the head forwards and bring the hands forwards', etc.) but all that is said explicitly about voice quality is that a puppet's voice quality should match its physiognomy and serve to make its voice distinct from that of other puppets, by whatever means:

> Finding the voices of your puppets requires long training. Begin by finding the voice that fits the puppet. Look at him, put your mouth in the same position as the puppet, think of the timbre his voice might have, and usually you will find the voice without too much trouble. When two puppets have to engage in dialogue, the voices have to be quite distinct. You can contrast a high and a low voice, a clear and a muddy voice, you can speak as though you have a hot potato in your mouth, bring your lower lip far forwards, and so on. (Meilink, 1953: 38)

In the absence of a 'system' of voice quality, voice quality can be made to mean on the basis of provenance and on the basis of experiential meaning potential. The first occurs when people adopt a fashionable accent or imitate the voice of a movie star or other celebrity. The second involves the material qualities of the voice, and their meaning potential, derived from what you *do* when you produce a voice that displays those qualities. We will discuss a few of them here, just as we did with the material qualities of plastic (a more extensive discussion of this subject can be found in Van Leeuwen, 1999).

Tension

Tension is an experience we all have in common. Something happens to your voice when you tense the muscles of your throat. As the lower overtones are reduced and the higher overtones increased, the voice becomes higher, sharper and brighter. We also know *when* this tends to happen – when we are angry, excited, nervous, and so on. On these kinds of knowledge the meaning potential of tension is founded, but what exactly tension will mean in any specific instance of course depends on context and on the other vocal qualities with which it may combine.

Tension can be an overall characteristic of certain styles of singing, for instance in rock. In his overview of singing styles across the world, Lomax says that tension often accompanies the singing of women in societies where there is a great deal of sexual repression (early marriages, severe sanctions for female adulterers, and so on):

> It is as if it is one of the assignments of the favoured singer to act out the level of sexual tension which the customs of society establish as normal. The content of this message may be painful and anxiety-producing, but the effect upon the culture member may be stimulating, erotic and pleasurable, since the song reminds him of familiar sexual emotions and experiences. (Lomax, 1968: 194)

Roughness

A second aspect of voice quality is one we have already touched on: roughness, voices in which we can hear other things besides the tone of the voice itself – friction sounds, hoarseness, harshness, rasp. Much of its effect results from the a-periodic vibration of the vocal chords which cause noise in the spectrum (Laver, 1980: 128). As this is more audible in the lower pitches it is more easily heard in male voices, and as a result rough voices are common in male speech and singing.

Breathiness

In breathiness there is also an extraneous sound mixed in with the tone of the voice – breath. Inevitably the voice is at the same time also soft, and, as already mentioned, breathiness can therefore be associated with sensuality, intimacy, etc.

Loudness range

The loudness range of the voice is most crucially associated with distance, the ability of the voice to cover a large territory. As a result vocal loudness is strongly related to power and domination. The loud voice claims most territory, whereas the soft voice excludes all but a few others, and is therefore associated with intimacy, confidentiality and so on.

Pitch range

The scale from the very low 'in the chest' voice to the very high voice relates to gender in complex ways. Men use the higher regions of their pitch range to dominate and assert – only the very highest voices, e.g. counter tenor, can become ambiguous in gender terms. A man who speaks low is usually not trying to dominate, but making himself small by mumbling a bit – the booming bass is the exception, and often considered a bit overbearing. Women, on the other hand, use the lower end of their pitch range to be assertive. This is difficult to do, however, without at the same time increasing loudness and so women are faced with a dilemma. Either they speak low (which is assertive) and soft (which is intimate), with which they risk invoking the 'dangerous woman' stereotype, or they speak high (thus 'belittling' themselves) and loud (thus being assertive), which can invoke the stereotype of the shrill and strident 'fishwife'. In either case the dominant norms of the public, assertive 'masculine' voice will be at odds with the dominant norms of the private, intimate ('feminine') voice. Poynton (1996: 8) recalls that

> In 1970s Tasmania the same person who represented herself as 'Patricia Hughes' using a dark voice (the voice of authority) in reading the news on the Tasmanian 'highbrow' station 7ZL became 'Patti, your Thursday bird' using a lighter, hyper-feminised voice to introduce herself on the 'popular' station 7ZR.

Similarly, in the movies there are women stereotyped as the 'innocent, vulnerable girl next door', who seduces with a high, childish voice (Marilyn Monroe), and women stereotyped as dark and dangerous temptresses who seduce with low, sensuous voices (Lauren Bacall). Shepherd describes a particular singing style as the style of 'woman as emotional nurturer': the voice is soft and warm, with an open throat, and relatively low:

> The typical sound of woman-as-sex-object involves a similar comparison. The softer, warmer, hollower tones of the woman singer as emotional nurturer become closed off with a certain edge, a certain vocal sheen that is quite different from the male-appropriated hard core of timbre typical of 'cock' rock. Tones such as those produced by Shirley Bassey in 'Big Spender', for instance, are essentially head tones, and it could in this sense be argued that the transition from woman the nurturer to woman the sex object represents a shift, physiologically coded, from the 'feminine heart' to the 'masculine head'. (Shepherd, 1991: 167–8)

Vibrato

Finally, the voice may be plain and unwavering or have some kind or regular or irregular 'vibrato'. This again means what it is. The 'vibrato' sound literally and figuratively trembles, and the semiotic value of that derives again from the kinds of things that may make us tremble, that is, from our emotions. This brings us to a another source of gender stereotypes, namely that the female voice is more emotional. This can come out through vibrato, but also through the use of an increased pitch range. McConnell-Ginet (1977) says that women use a wider pitch range and more rapid and frequent changes of pitch than men. In Anglo-American cultures women (and children) are given more licence to show their emotions than men, and this has an impact also on the vocal style: 'Part of women's being emotional in our culture derives from our *sounding* emotional' (McConnell-Ginet, 1977: 77).

Let us finally look at an instance of the use of these material qualities, the singing voice of Madonna. The example is discussed at greater length in Van Leeuwen (1999). A semiotic analysis of the gendered meanings of the music of one of the songs we discuss can be found in McClary (1991).

The first song we will discuss is 'Like A Virgin'. In the first verse and chorus, in terms of the features we have discussed here, Madonna's voice is tense, loud, high, smooth, non-breathy and has some vibrato. In other words, she uses a kind of 'little girl' voice (high, smooth) but at the same time mixes in a certain stridence (tense, loud): in other words, the 'little girl', so 'shiny and new', also bears the scars of abuse and betrayal.

The second song is 'Live to Tell'. Again, in the first verse and chorus, Madonna's voice changes midway through the song. She starts in a voice which is quite different from the one she used in 'Like a Virgin': less high, less tense, lower, more relaxed, more sure of itself, and also breathier and warmer. Only after a while (at 'a man can tell ...') is there a change. Occasional vibrato and increased tension add the intensity of a re-lived emotional experience to some of the key moments of the verse. And the accompaniment also changes. Two other (instrumental) voices join in, as though representing two other women with the same or similar experiences, one a tense, high voice, playing around the melody in staccato notes, the other a more strident and sustained voice which doubles the melody.

Thus the sound of Madonna's voice embodies different versions of modern woman, and 'tells a tale' of the contradictory values contemporary women must live and the contradictory images and identities they must cope with and embody.

5 Distribution

Media of preservation and distribution

Erving Goffman's theory of 'footing' (1981) describes the various layers of the 'participation framework' and 'production format' of talk. The layers of his 'production format' correspond closely to the linguistic strata of semantics, lexicogrammar and phonology (or 'meaning', 'wording' and 'sounding', as Halliday puts it, 1985), but rather than seeing them as strata, as layers of language, Goffman sees them as divisions of semiotic labour. His 'participation framework', similarly, defines recipient roles in terms of different modes of participating in the communicative event. In the production of talk, the 'principal' is the person (or institution) 'whose beliefs are told', 'whose position is established', the 'author' is the person who 'selects the sentiments that are being expressed and the words in which they are encoded', and the 'animator' is the 'sounding box in use' (1981: 144). The three functions can be combined in one person, but other configurations are also possible. When a speech-writer writes the words a politician will deliver, the speech-writer is 'author' only, and the politician both 'principal' and 'animator'. When an actor interprets the words of a play, the actor is 'animator' and the playwright both 'principal' and 'author'. When a BBC newsreader reads the news, the BBC is 'principal', the newswriter 'author' and the newsreader 'animator'.

Clearly Goffman's account corresponds closely to our distinction between 'discourse', 'design' and 'production', not only because we use the same kind of criteria to distinguish the 'layers', but also because we see each layer as realised, not just in the 'text', but also in the organisation of the social practice of which the text is part. The main difference is that we extend this idea to all semiotic modes, and that we see 'production' not just as 'execution' and the 'animator' not as just as a 'sounding box'. The 'animator' (or 'producer', in our terms) is vitally involved in the production of meaning, even in contexts which split up the jobs of 'designing/authoring' and 'production', and require 'producers' to 'execute' instructions – scores, scripts, blueprints, recipes, and so on. In the case of newsreading, for instance, newsreaders do not just refrain from interpretation, they actively signify the impartiality of the news through the way they sound – through their even stresses, stylised rhythms, ritualised modes of phrasing, and so on (Van Leeuwen, 1984, 1999). Cooks, as 'producers' of meals, know that following a recipe, following someone else's 'design of a meal', always involves interpretation, even when they try to stick to the recipe rather than just use it as a point of departure.

When discussing 'animators', Goffman notes that they sometimes 'share this physical function with a loudspeaker system or telephone'. He does not coin a term for this role or invoke the people who may, for instance, operate the amplifier or connect you with the person you want to speak to, but clearly there is another role here, the role of 'encoder/ transmitter', a role which always involves technology, and may be automatised, performed by a machine, as is today often the case with the telephone, or involve a human operator as part of the semiotic chain. In Chapter 1 we referred to this layer as 'distribution', and noted that distribution refers to the technical 're-coding' of semiotic products and events, for purposes of recording (e.g. tape recording, digital recording) and/or distribution (e.g. telephony, radio and television transmission). We also noted that distribution technologies are generally invented for purposes of re-production (we will have to qualify this later in the chapter), but may nevertheless acquire a semiotic potential of their own, as with the loudspeaker, which does not only allow the speaker to be heard across greater distance (a matter of pure 'distribution'), but also opens up new semiotic choices, such as choice of microphone distance, which can, for instance, signify intimacy in a context where formerly only formal, public modes of address would have been possible (Van Leeuwen, 1999). New 'production formats' emerge as a result. The composer Brian Eno called the sound studio 'a compositional tool' (1983: 56). By working directly with tape loops to create rhythms and textures, he became designer, producer and technical encoder all in one. And composers are of course also the 'principals' of their work, unless it is, for instance, commissioned film music, where the producer and/or director of the film would be the 'principal'. In film production, likewise, the job of recording has become much more than that, though until recently only in the case of the image. Camera work is split up into the roles of a visual 'designer', or director of photography (DOP), who does not him/herself operate the camera, and a gaffer (chief lighting technician) and camera operator (each with with several assistants) who 'execute' the design according to the DOP's instructions (in smaller productions several or all of these roles might be conflated). The highest ranking sound recordist, on the other hand, is called simply that, 'recordist' (or 'engineer'), and operates the equipment him/herself. In the last twenty years or so, however, Hollywood's approach to sound has become much more creative, and sound recordists are now in fact often referred to as 'sound designers' (Van Leeuwen, 1999). The contribution of the film laboratory, on the other hand, has remained purely technical. Where it affects 'design' and 'production', such as in the matter of colour, laboratory technicians such as the 'colour grader' work under direction of the DOP.

The two aspects of 'distribution', 're-encoding' (recording) and 'transmitting', are in principle separate, although they can of course also be combined. Telephone conversations are only transmitted, and films or compact discs only recorded – if they are also to be transmitted, another re-encoding will have to occur, for the purpose of broadcasting the film or the CD, for instance. The computer on the other hand can transmit and record (file) email messages in one operation. Until now, it has mainly been in the area of recording, rather than also in the area of transmission, that the role of the technical 're-encoder' could become conflated with that of the producer, or even that of the designer. But in the age of the internet this is changing. Transmission allows networking, and networking has become a major cultural preoccupation, whether to allow distance conferencing or game playing, or, for instance, to allow musicians who are not physically together in the same place to improvise a piece of music together. As we will discuss below, this is now moving beyond '*re*-production' and is extending the semiotic resources for the production of interactive meanings in many contexts.

Distribution as message

In the most highly valued cultural traditions of Western Europe, 'producers' have to execute faithfully the instructions (scripts, scores, blueprints, etc.) of designers, or at best, interpret them in accordance with an explicitly elaborated reconstruction of the intentions of the designer. In 'classical' music, musicians follow the score written by the composer, and obey the instructions of the conductor – neither composers nor conductors need to touch actual musical instruments. In the theatre, actors say the lines written by the playwright, and, again, follow the instructions of a director. In architecture, builders work to the blueprints of the architect. And as we have seen, in film the DOP designs the way the image will be photographed, but does not need to touch the lights or the camera him/herself. Such designers enjoy a much higher status than the producers who do the actual work, and they receive greater rewards as well.

It is the same with the encoder and the transmitter. Here, too, it has been of fundamental importance that the traditionally most highly regarded cultural forms should be seen to *re*-code an original, as faithfully as possible, to leave that original untouched, and to make it well-nigh impossible to tell reproduction and original apart. We have already quoted the EMI producer who said 'I want to make records which will sound in the public's home exactly like what it would hear in the best seat in an acoustically perfect hall' (Walter Legge, quoted in Chanan, 1995: 133). Just how different the reproduction is from the original, just how many dimensions of sensory experience it lacks, and how many elements of 'noise' it adds, is then conveniently forgotten – until the next technical improvement comes along, and we can suddenly no longer disattend the scratching of the record or the absence of colour which, only yesterday, did not trouble us.

'Distribution' has produced enormous gains in accessibility – first of the printed word, later also of pictorial art, music, and drama, all of which we can now buy and take home in the form of reproductions and recordings, or have transmitted to our homes in the way in which we also receive water, gas and electricity. Despite all this, many people have also experienced a sense of loss, perhaps especially those who have something to lose, who do not gain from this increased accessibility anything they did not already have before. This loss is felt, above all, as a loss of embodiment, a loss of presence, a loss of 'aura', and as a loss of context, of the ties with a specific place and a unique moment in time that can never be repeated and registers vividly in all our senses. Plato, in the *Phaedrus*, said about writing, that most vital and, at the time, new re-coding medium, that it missed what today we would call interactivity and destroyed the faculty of memory. Erasmus would echo this much later with respect to print. Walter Benjamin commented on the more recent photographic re-codings of art and drama in his famous essay 'The Work of Art in the Age of Mechanical Reproduction', where he describes how 'the cathedral leaves its locale to be received in the studio of a lover of art' and how 'the choral production, performed in an auditorium or in the open air, resounds in the drawing room' and concludes that 'the situations into which the product of mechanical reproduction can be brought may not touch the actual work of art, yet the quality of its presence is always depreciated' (1977: 223). Baudrillard, in a similar vein, compares the pre-industrial object and the industrial 'serial object', and finds that 'finish is wanting, as is inventiveness. Faithfully transposed as they may be, forms suffer a subtle loss of their originality' (1996: 147). As a result of this loss, the semiotic object no longer means-in-context, whether that context is Benjamin's drawing room (or the walkman), or an imitation Louis XV chair in a modern flat. It must now mean-of-itself, in a new context, and is thus open to multiple interpretation, only reined in, to different degrees, by the contemporary proliferation of hermeneutic regimes that reach us in many different formats and through many different channels – in the case of art, for instance, through reviews, critiques, interviews and biographies aimed at a range of levels and informed by a range of different discourses; and in the case of furniture, for instance, through furniture catalogues, 'Good Living' type magazines, TV programmes and websites, and, indeed, accounts of interior design by philosophers like Baudrillard.

Another loss is the loss of multimodality itself. Recoding always involves reduction, even if we often forget or no longer value what has been eliminated by this reduction. This is most clearly so in the case of scripts. Western music notation does not notate what voices and instruments should actually *sound* like, or how they should actually articulate the notes, for instance. And writing, as Canadian composer Murray Schafer said, loses the 'music of speech': 'How do we break language out of its print sarcophagus? How do we smash the grey coffins of muttering and let the words howl off the page like spirits possessed?' (1986: 199). But it is also true for recordings and 'serial objects'. Film and television drama loses not only the physical presence of the actor, but also the third dimension, and the sense of smell and touch and taste. Baudrillard's 'serial objects' reproduce colour and form, but they lose some key dimensions of 'original' materiality:

> The glass partition of a model interior will have a plastic echo in the serial version. Solid wood furniture will reappear in whitewood veneer. A fine woollen or wild-silk dress will proliferate in ready-to-wear form in a wool mixture or rayon. It is the heft, hardiness, grain, 'warmth' of a material whose presence or absence serves as a mark of difference. Such tactile qualities are close to the most profound defining qualities of the model – far more so than the visual values of colour and form. (1996: 147)

The loss is most strongly felt when familiar contents are packaged in new media, when the wide-screen film is viewed on the small screen, or the book read on the computer screen. And, as McLuhan noted (1966), this is often the case: new media initially tend to repackage old media. Writing often purported to record the spoken word, as in the Old Testament, where many books begin by establishing themselves as records of speech: 'The Lord called Moses, and spoke to him, saying ...' (Leviticus 1:1), 'These are the words that Moses spoke to all Israel ...' (Deuteronomy 1:1). In the New Testament, on the other hand, we have entered the age of writing: 'It seemed good to me to write an orderly account for you, most excellent Theophilus, that you may know the truth concerning the things of which you have been informed' (Luke 1:3–4), but the teachings of Christ of which Luke writes are still oral teachings. Many of the contents of today's digital media are once again those of the media that preceded them – the encyclopedia, the magazine, the catalogue, the scientific paper.

But others may feel, as acutely, a sense of gain, a fascination with the new, and this is in the first place a fascination, not with the content, but with the message constituted by the arrival of the new medium itself, to again invoke McLuhan (1966). New media are not invented to meet needs already adequately catered for. They are invented to meet new needs. Often these are quite specialised needs, arising within the military, government, industry, science. Thus writing came about in connection with the construction of great temples in Mesopotamia, projects for which old mnemonic techniques were no longer adequate and which required new ways of keeping records and accounts (Coulmas, 1989). The institutions creating such new technologies have power and cultural prestige. Anyone with a large or small stake in the future will take note and perhaps want to emulate them. As a result new technologies will be adopted even in areas where the old ways of doing things are still functioning well. In this way the medium's message is spread – in the case of writing, for instance, its power of temporally and spatially extending the reach of the word, its ability to extend memory, the permanence of its authority, and the technical and legal precision it allows, in short, the 'restructuring of consciousness' it brings about (Ong, 1982).

Similar stories can be told about other media. Photography was first used by Thomas Wedgwood, in 1800, to 'copy outline and shades of paintings, or profiles of figures procured by the agency of light' (quoted in Coe, 1977: 13), and, a little later, by the artist Niepce and the scenic painter Daguerre as aids for more realistic representation in paintings and scenic backdrops. Yet a wider motif informed the work of these inventors, even if they may not have been consciously aware of it. Before having found a social use, before having been invented even, photography already was a new and radical concept for disengaging the visual aspect of people, places and things from their time and place, and, therefore, for making them manipulable, transportable and controllable. The decontextualisation deplored by Benjamin was also the message of the medium of photography, and the reason for people's fascination with it. As described by Coe (1977), people soon began to keep portraits of distant loved ones in ornately embossed leather cases, in albums with covers of mother-of-pearl, Japanese lacquer or carved wood, and with built-in clocks or music boxes that tinkled as the pages were turned. They mounted photographs in jewellery, lockets, pendants, rings, tie-pins and cufflinks, exactly as now proposed with respect to the so-called 'wearable computer'. Ornate stereoscopes, mounted on columns, brought pictures of exotic places into people's homes, so that all could join in the spirit of Imperialism. People were fascinated with the medium, even before it had fully found its place in society 'as an item for exhibition, a record for scrutiny, a target for surveillance' (Sontag, 1977: 156). In this way they could absorb the message, the new consciousness which photography would bring, participate in the power of decontextualisation, and learn about the power of appearances, of judging people, places and things by what they *look* like.

In the same way radio was invented for the relatively limited purpose of two-way, ship to shore and military communication, and did not find its place as a broadcasting medium until almost thirty years after its invention. But during all that time the public remained fascinated with the new medium – there were demonstrations, such as Lee DeForest's broadcast from the Eiffel Tower in 1908, heard 500 miles from Paris (Barnouw, 1966), and there were the many thousands of amateurs who made, not only their own receivers, but also their own transmission sets, and who played records, read poems, made speeches, or simply chatted to each other on air, again, exactly as is done today on the internet. Yet broadcasting (and with it the decline of radio as a two-way medium of communication) did not come about until there were more compelling social, political and economic reasons for it, in the 1920s, when the motor car and rail transport had allowed cities to expand to a point where traditional forms of public communication were no longer possible, and where, as Raymond Williams memorably described it, 'the centre of interest was for the first time the family home, where men and women stared from its windows, or waited anxiously for messages, to learn about forces "out there" which could determine the conditions of their lives' (1974: 27). Similar patterns can now be observed with respect to the internet, which began as a means of communication for the military and for scientists, and is now an object of major public fascination, even though it has not yet managed to supplant older forms (or to make a profit for the companies that already use it).

The message of the medium, then, is not one: it spells the end of one form of consciousness and the beginning of another, and it depends on your interest, on who you are and what you do, what will put most weight in the scale, the things that were or the things that will be, the losses or the gains. But what is lost may return, and what is gained may yet turn out to be a loss. The new technologies' emphasis on multimodality, three-dimensionality and interactivity can be seen as a return of many of the things that were lost in the transition from 'orality' to 'literacy', as a 'secondary orality', in other words (Ong, 1977). But the search for immersion, 3D virtual reality and interactivity, and the advent of 'cyberculture', may also signify the most profound loss of embodiment we have seen yet – a theme to which we will return later in this chapter.

Distribution as 'language'

It stands to reason that an exploration of new media for the preservation or transmission of texts and communicative events begins with the media themselves – with their magic, with the possibilities they suddenly open: I can photograph a fleeting moment and take it home, keep it, study it at leisure; I can receive articles and books via a cable, rather than having to buy them in a bookshop or order them from a publisher. Nor is it surprising that another question immediately follows: what effect will this have on my life, and on society at large? These are the two key questions of many of the debates: the potential of the new technology (rather than what is actually done with it, which, initially, is usually much less exciting), and its impact, its effect on society and on individuals. These are also the questions we have looked at so far. But when new technologies move beyond the stage of recoding or transmitting already existing 'content', when they begin to develop a semiotic potential of their own, the technological element recedes into the background. In writing, for instance, 'production' and 'distribution' have fully merged. Writing has become, not a recoding, but an originating medium, itself the object of further recodings such as print, and now the computer screen (hence the 'auratic' value of manuscripts). In other cases, like film and photography, both elements are still discernible, and both should be kept in view. But these media, too, increasingly become 'manuscript media', to be stored and transmitted in digital form. Even the digital technologies themselves should be looked at from a social semiotic point of view, as they already begin to move away from their 'manuscript media', and start to create their own forms.

Speaking about 'distribution' *semiotically* means, in the first place, acknowledging that the technologies may be used in the service of preservation and transmission as well as in the service of *transforming* what is recorded or transmitted, of creating new representations and interactions, rather than extending the reach of existing ones. It also means acknowledging that this is not an either/or distinction but a sliding scale. On one end of the scale is the 'faithful recording', for instance the music record which positions the listener in the best seat of the auditorium, just as the earliest films positioned the viewer in the best seat of the theatre. Closely related to this are instances which still pretend to such faithfulness, but have in fact already left it behind. Here is an example. A track from a French 'ambient sounds' recording by Eloisa Mathieu, *Ambient Sounds at Costa-Rica: Afternoon at the La Selva Biological Station*, has three distinct groups of sound: first, the sound of cicadas, a continuous drone; second, a variety of birdcalls, more discrete individual sounds in other words, which nevertheless continue without noticeable gaps throughout the track; and third, entering only later, the cry of a single howler monkey. The sleeve notes state that sound mixer Jean Roche 'had the task of mixing the recordings, to recreate atmospheres unique to each habitat'. But Roche did more than that. To anyone who has heard the deafening noise of cicadas on a summer afternoon it is immediately clear that the level of the cicadas on this track is far too low relative to the other sounds, and it is equally clear that the aural point of view created by the mix (the equivalent to 'the best seat in the auditorium') is physically impossible. No one could simultaneously be so close to so many different birds that the sound of each and every one of them would dominate that of the cicadas to the extent it does on the track – and then be closer still to the howler monkey. This is not a faithful recreation of the sounds of the forest, not the recording of an original event, it is a transformation which creates a new order amongst these sounds, an order that is actually very much like the soundscape experienced in modern cities: a background hum (the ever-present sound of the city), occasional 'middle ground' individual sounds (say the people and cars passing through our street), and the close foreground sounds we consciously attend to (say someone walking next to me, and talking to me). In this context the different animal sounds create a social hierarchy, that of the thousands of strangers I will never know, indistinguishable from each other so far as I am concerned (the social background of my life); the people I recognise, e.g. neighbours, people in the shops (the social middle ground of my life); and those I relate closely with (the social foreground of my life).

Further down the scale there is no longer any attempt to disguise the physical impossibility of the subject position created by the mix. Mixing is used as another musical instrument, and a work is created that can only have existence in the technical medium. This is the case, for example, in modern 'drum 'n' bass' dance music. Tracks such as Art of Noise's 'Something Always Happens', Love Corporation's 'Give Me Some Love', or Dual Fusion's 'Anything Goes' reverse the hierarchy of traditional European music, and put the 'melody' in the background and the 'accompaniment' in the foreground. Closest are the complex and shifting rhythms of the drums and the bass, the drums with the breakbeat, a clean, clear and close rustle of snare drum taps, sticks on closed hihats and so on, the bass at a more steady tempo, with short, deep and dampened notes. Both drums and bass sound in fact as though they are not played in an actual space at all, but resonate inside the head or the body. Somewhat further along there is some kind of keyboard sound, an organ playing sustained chords that alternate rather than progress, or a piano playing repetitive patterns that shift from one phase into another every once in a while. Furthest away are intermittent snippets of sound, natural and 'techno' sound effects, voices, fragments sampled from the history of black music – all very soft, very distant, completely backgrounded by the prominent rhythms in the foreground. This change in emphasis from melody to rhythm is a crucial change, a change from listening to participating, from being an audience to being a community. Melodies are phrased in the same way as speech, and they are sung or played by a solo voice or a group in unison. As such they are very much like speech – musical *messages,* addressed to listeners, to an audience. Rhythms, on the other hand, are continuous, like human activities such as walking or hammering or sawing, and form a background for action, whether the communicative action of singing a melody or some other action, as in worksong or walkman. In drum 'n' bass music, participating in a physical activity becomes foreground, the thing to attend to, and speech (message, meaning) becomes the background. The music fan changes from an individual admiring stars who perform on a distant stage and imaginarily identifying with them while more or less confined to a chair in an auditorium, to a member of a group actively participating in the physical group activity of dancing while surrounded by music. Walter Benjamin stressed the effect of 'distraction', a form of attending to something which involves both 'use' and 'perception', both 'touch' and 'sight', as occurs when we walk through a building in which we have business, and as such is radically different from the 'attentive concentration of a tourist before a famous building'. He sees watching film as governed by this: 'Reception in a state of distraction, which is increasingly noticeable in all fields of art and is symptomatic of profound changes in apperception, finds in the film its true means of exercise' (1977: 242). The change in music perception noted here is of a similar kind – and also achieved through a semiotically oriented, rather than a recording-oriented use of technology, in this case mixing instead of editing.

The issue of 'recording' versus 'transformation' has been a key issue in film theory. Initially, many theorists, most notably Bazin and Kracauer, saw 'recording' as the essence of the medium. For Kracauer 'an impersonal, completely artless camera record is aesthetically irreproachable in film' (1960: 13); in other words, artistic value is, paradoxically, guaranteed by the 'artless' recording ethos. He approvingly cites the photographic historian Beaumont Newhall, who praises the 'intrinsic beauty of aerial serial photographs taken with automatic cameras during the war for military purposes' (1960: 14). The constructivist film-makers of the 1920s and critics like Arnheim (1957), on the other hand, argued that it is the medium's shortcomings as a recording medium, the ways in which it *reduces* what it records, which allow it to develop a new semiotic and artistic potential. The absence of the third dimension, the absence of colour (in the black-and-white era), the absence of time–space continuum, and the absence of the non-visual world of the senses are not a loss, but a gain: 'Only gradually ... the possibility of utilising the difference between film and real life for the purpose of making formally significant images was realised', writes Arnheim (1957: 42). Although this sounds very formalistic, his examples show that he saw 'the difference between film and real life' as also and at the same time used semiotically, with 'artistic use of reduced depth' allowing, for instance, a 'symbolic rearrangement of the natural proportions' (1957: 63), as in Eisenstein's *The General Line*, which has a shot of a bookkeeper in which 'the ledger is enormous and the man writing in it quite small' so as to 'depict a bureaucratic office set-up, in which red tape obstructs any reasonable conduct of affairs' (1957: 63). Here a meaning is expressed, not through the productive work of the set designer or the actor, but through the productive work of the image designer.

Even unintended or unwanted transformations can become signifiers. The scratches on old film prints distract from the illusion of reality, as do the discolorations that occur in old colour prints. Both have now become key signifiers of 'period', and can even be added digitally. Young artists use such signifiers in producing video art, or they produce music consisting entirely of the 'unwanted' noises produced by gramophone records. On the other hand, the recording ethos continues in the newest media, as we noted at a conference, when the director of a German music archive spoke of the conservation of records in digital form, without even being willing to consider that this conservation might also be a transformation (no museum would dream of 'preserving' clay tablets in print form).

Further along the scale there is no longer an original to 'recode': our scale in fact runs from 'faithful recoding' (transcribing, copying, recording, simulating, imitating, reconstructing – the multiplicity of terms testifies to its continued importance), via transformation (adapting, re-packaging, 'digest-ing', etc.) to origination, the point at which distribution and production merge. Midway between transformation and origination we find editing. It was due to editing that film could develop its own semiotic potential, become a 'language'. Benjamin already saw how editing deprived actors of creating their performances as an 'integrated whole' and yet allowed the result to appear 'seamless' (1977: 230). Editing can in fact take over parts of the actors' work (their orientation towards people and things, for instance, and their timing), and even build a performance out of shots of people who are not actors at all and were not acting when the shots were taken: the Russian constructivist film-makers demonstrated this already in the early 1920s, for instance in the famous 'Kuleshov experiments'. But the principles of editing are not restricted to film. A form of editing is possible in the production of 'serial objects', where, as Baudrillard says, 'style gives way to combination' and objects become a 'conglomeration of details' (1996: 147–8). In music, 'recordings' can be produced by assembling tracks which may have been made days apart, or not even recorded for the particular record or CD assembled, as in contemporary dance music. The technology which makes this possible is sampling, and its various uses occupy different points on our scale. Goodwin (1988) distinguished three: 'realist' sampling, aiming at imitating a particular instrument, and hence similar to our 'faithful recoding'; 'modernist' sampling, which leaves the original intact as an integrated whole, but inserts ironised or satirised quotes from other works; and 'postmodernist' sampling, which creates works from pre-existing materials without placing them in quotation marks, as it were.

A similar trend towards 'editing' can be seen in children's construction toys. Where children were once given building blocks with which they could create objects they could then assemble into scenes and play with, companies such as Lego now increasingly provide children with ready-made objects to assemble into scenes and play with. In writing, too, editing is increasingly common. One of us worked as a scriptwriter before the arrival of the word-processor. During script meetings with the producer, director and script editor, his writing was literally cut into strips so that paragraphs and lines of dialogue could be glued together in a new order, together with new bits of writing, typed on the spot. Other people discovered this way of writing only after the arrival of the word-processor.

Still further along the scale there are not even original fragments any more. Production and distribution merge. The recoding medium becomes an originating medium and does not recode anything else any more, just as the written word, in the end, no longer recoded speech, at least in many of its uses – writing continued to be used for the transcription of speech as well, and a few of its other uses (e.g. lists) had never recoded another medium, but that is true of other 'recoding' media as well. In music, synthesisers moved from the imitation of different organ voices or of instruments like the harpsichord or the string section of the orchestra, to synthesising wholly new sounds. A revolutionary new instrument, the MIDI (Musical Instrument Digital Interface), combined the synthesiser with a sequencer and allowed the two to interact with each other as well as with other micro-processors. Thus it became possible to create music directly on the computer, by feeding a traditional written score into the machine, or by playing music into the machine and then creating new settings for instrumental texture, tempo and so on, or by keying it in note by note (see for example Durant, 1990). The London group AudioRom produces a CD-ROM on which multi-layered music can be created using only a computer mouse to select options on a visual interface, so that writing music or playing a keyboard is no longer necessary. In the area of film, sets may now be created directly on the computer, and technology for sampling actors and then creating their performances on the computer ('synthespians') are in development.

One further aspect needs to be discussed, the nature and meaning of the recoding codes themselves. All 'recoding' media build up reproductions, productions and transmissions out of their own 'primitives', their own minimal units. The primitives of photography, for instance, are silverhalide grains, in the case of colour film coupled with dyes in one of three basic colours, yellow, magenta and cyan. When photography and film are used naturalistically, the grain is to remain invisible. But just as the microscope can reveal teeming life in apparently clear water, so the magnified photographic image can reveal a primeval chaos of grains, clustered together or spaced apart without any apparent order, a world without meaning, beneath the familiar, recognisable world of everyday appearances (*see* Fig. 5.1). Impressionist painters made this new code visible by encoding the visible world in coloured specks of light, clustering together to form recognisable colours and shapes which would dissolve into specks of coloured light again if the viewer were to move too close (*see* Fig. 5.2). While the new medium of photography was used in the service of old content and old modes of representation, the old medium of painting drew attention to the new code, the new key for representing the world. Artists would remain fascinated by that moment when marks on paper or canvas suddenly acquire representational value, or representations suddenly become meaningless marks (e.g. Richard Hamilton's *Margate* series, or Antonioni's *Blow Up*, both from 1966).

When the pixel of the video image is magnified, something totally different emerges, an ordered world of neatly coloured rectangles, 'not unlike the grid of the draughtsman who wishes to break down the impossible infinity of information into manageable units' (Flint, 1999a: 2). In 'analogue' video images there still are fuzzy boundaries between the rectangles, but digital video resolves this fuzziness (*see* Fig. 5.3). All the rectangles become squares and the lines between them are sharply delineated. Like photographic images, video images, whether digital or analogue, are mostly used naturalistically, and this means that the angularity of the pixels must be repressed. But painters, again, have brought it out into the open. An enlarged section of an analogue video image can look remarkably like a 'suprematist composition' by Malevitch (Fig. 5.4). Mondrian used coloured rectangles as his basic building blocks, and attempted to 'abstract the curve' in exactly the way video images do, though on a much magnified scale: 'In painting a tree, I progressively abstracted the curve; you can understand that very little "tree" remained' (quoted in Jaffé, 1986: 120). One of our students, Robert Flint, to whose research these paragraphs owe a great deal and who uses these ideas in his own work as a video artist, drew our attention to the work of Sarah Morris, whose paintings use a sharply delineated grid of squares and a few flat colours to represent people and places (Flint, 1999b). And the 'pixel principle' is

Figure 5.1 *Photographic grain*

Figure 5.2 *Georges Seurat,* The Parade of the Circus

Figure 5.3 *Enlarged pixels of digital video image (from experimental video by Scopac,* Cyan on Magenta, *1999)*

applied in other areas of culture too. Construction games like Lego use brightly coloured rectangular blocks and therefore make it quite difficult to create curved surfaces, especially on a small scale. The 'pixel principle' is more than a convenient technical recoding format, it is a key concept for understanding how our world is constituted, taught to children from a very young age.

We will now summarise the main points made so far.

Preservation

Distribution technologies start out as 'preservation' and/or 'transmission' technologies, although there may be other, usually more limited, 'original' functions as well. If preservation technologies move from 'faithful recoding' towards synthesis, towards developing a semiotic potential of their own, it will be particularly in the area of representation.

Transmission

Transmission technologies increase spatial reach and thereby decrease distance, whether on a small scale (e.g. the loudspeaker) or on a large scale (e.g. satellite TV). They affect interactive, rather than representational meaning, first because their very

Figure 5.4 *Kasimir Malevitch,* Black Square and Red Square *(1913)*

nature as a technology has the potential to make us relate to each other in different ways, and second because the semiotic potentials they develop also tend to be in the area of interactive meaning (e.g. microphone distance). While technologies may facilitate either preservation or transmission, or both, semiotic products and events themselves always have both representational and interactive meanings, even though one or the other may dominate in specific cases.

We shall now discuss some of our terms in order to recapitulate the main points from this section.

Recapitulation

Transcription: Transcription, whether through manual copying, recording, mass production, imitation or other methods, and whether resulting in a single 're-production' or a large number of 'copies', always involves an attempt to be as faithful as possible to a semiotic product or event articulated in *another* medium. This ideal may not ever be reached, but is nevertheless striven for, even in areas such as modern image synthesis, which does not yet envisage creating wholly new visual objects in the way electronic instruments have created wholly new sounds.

Adaptation: In the case of adaptation there is still an original semiotic object or event to be recoded, and often an attempt at faithfulness to that original. But a need for adaptation to another context – another length, another format, another medium, another type of audience – is also recognised, and this requires transformation, whether it is the jungle adapted to the sensitivities of urban listeners, spoken dialogue adapted to the written novel, or an encyclopaedia adapted to the CD-ROM format.

Assembly: In the case of assembly there is no longer a single, integrated original. Instead, a range of fragments is assembled into a whole. The fragments are either produced for the purpose (as, still, in most films), or collected from a variety of sources (as in the compilation film or the collage), or something in between (as in many contemporary television documentaries).

Synthesis: Synthesis involves the generation of an original in a medium which had before been a recoding medium, but is now used to articulate semiotic products or events directly. It is at this point that distribution in fact becomes production, and ceases to exist as a separate layer.

We have tried to formulate these concepts in such a way that they can apply to a variety of semiotic objects and events, to music recordings as well as mass produced armchairs, and to email exchanges as well as television broadcasts. In the next section we will apply them to some examples from contemporary computer-based media.

Distribution in contemporary computer texts

Our first example is, at least at first sight, an example of adaptation – the adaptation of reference books to CD-ROMs. Although it is possible to digitise books 'as they are', this is not what is usually done. Multimedia designers (who combine design and programming skills, hence, in our terms, design, production and distribution) see the job as requiring creative adaptation to a medium which is *multimodal* and *interactive.* There *is* division of semiotic labour, but it is the division between 'content providers' and 'interface designers'. The latter design, not so much the shape of the actual information in the database, as the ways in which users can access it, and interact with it. This in fact moves beyond adaptation, because the information consists of fragments which have not been assembled for the users in the way they are in older media. The users themselves must assemble the fragments and determine their order and sequence, though within the limits and according to the principles set by the interface designers.

The so-called 'guide interface' was pioneered by a group of designers in the United States, Tim Oren, Gitta Salomon, Kristee Kreitman and Abbe Don, in 1988 (Oren *et al.*, 1990). They were concerned about the way users of educational databases failed to do their own 'assembling' adequately, and became disoriented, ending up just clicking aimlessly from screen to screen, in the way people might walk through an all too large art gallery, moving rapidly from room to room, only briefly glancing at the paintings, and stopping at random from time to time to look at one painting in a little more detail. This is not the best way of viewing if the aim of the exercise is to learn something. To counteract this effect, they decided to provide users with 'travel guides', who would lead the way and navigate them through the informational labyrinth in more or less coherent fashion. The database they were working with dealt with American history and was adapted from a nine-volume encyclopaedia into the kind of fragmented and more or less self-contained screens with short texts which the computer requires. In the first version, the guide interface gave users a choice of guide from a set of stock characters such as the 'Slave', the 'Indian', the 'Preacher', the 'Diplomat', etc. None of these characters knew the way in all of the database. They only knew as much of it as pertained to their own interest – the 'Slave', for instance, would guide the user towards topics related to slavery and abolition. In a later version the characters were given a biography – the 'Preacher', for instance, was now born in New York during the Reformist period, had been a left-winger for some time, became active in the Abolition movement, and later worked as a missionary in the Oklahoma Indian territory. This provided the guides with a broader range of interests and helped 'narrativise' the guided tour – by now the designers had decided that it was important to build narratives on top of the systematically organised database.

When the designers tested this interface on users, two things became obvious. First, instead of creating a balanced combination of what we have called adaptation and assembly, they had gone too far towards adaptation and not left enough room for assembling. Although they had wanted 'closure to reside with the users as they interact with the database' (Oren *et al.*, 1990: 377), they had in effect 're-linearised' the database. Users did not take the opportunity to explore and branch out, but meekly followed the guide. The result, they felt, was too much like television, and not interactive enough. Second, users wanted to know whether they were actually seeing and hearing the events from the guide's point of view, whether, for instance, they were actually getting a slave's point of view or not. They were not, of course, because the same screens were used by different 'guides' in different contexts. The information was not written from different points of view, it was only assembled according to different points of view.

Dangerous Creatures, a CD-ROM for children published by Microsoft in 1994, allows users to assemble the information in three different ways. They can treat the CD-ROM as an encyclopaedia, by using the alphabetically organised *index.* They can choose to explore particular *themes,* such as 'habitats', or 'weapons' (users then enter by first choosing a region and then an animal from that region, or first a type of weapon such as 'jaws' or 'fangs' and then an animal possessing that weapon), or they can use the guide interface. If they choose the latter, they get a screen on which pictures of the twelve guides are symmetrically arranged, with captions indicating the kinds of tours they can conduct, the kinds of sights they can show, the kinds of stories they can tell, and so on (e.g. 'Amazon Adventure', 'African Safari', 'Coral Reef Dive', 'Native American Stories', 'Tales from Asia', 'Aboriginal Dreamtime'). After selecting a guide, users are introduced to him or her on a new screen. This screen has a written text on the left and the guide on the right, hailing the viewer, and depicted against a 'wild' landscape. The text is not only written, but also spoken, except for the instruction to click on to the next screen, which is only spoken. Here are examples from two different tours:

> Amazon adventure
> *(excited male voice)*
> Welcome, gather round. Our paddlers are just about ready to take us on a bird-watching trip down the river into the Amazon rainforest where, if we're lucky, we'll see a flock of brilliant parrots on the wing. Click my button when you're ready to get underway.

Aboriginal dreamtime
(soft, soothing, young female voice)
Once upon a time, there were no computers – like the one you're using now – no books, no pens, no paper. There was no way to hold on to history, except by telling it, over and over. The Aboriginal people of Australia began doing that thirty thousand years ago, when they first came to Australia from Asia. Click my button to hear the first part of the story.

Before 'getting underway' or 'hearing the first part of the story', users may call up the guide's 'CV', which will give them information about his or her education, favourite colours, favourite foods, hobbies, professional association, and also reveal a 'cool fact' (in the case of the Aboriginal storyteller that she 'has been seen in several places at once'). From this construction of the role and identity of the guide the young users of *Dangerous Creatures* will learn that the teller of the Native American stories, the Asian stories, the Aboriginal Dreamtime stories and the African stories has only one voice, and that this is not the voice of an old woman, but a smooth, young, and very professional voice, without a trace of accent. In Goffman's terms, she is only the 'animator' and not also the 'principal' and 'author' of the stories. They will also receive a lesson in multimodality: images create similarity and sound difference. Visually the tours are remarkably similar. The twelve guide introduction screens and CV screens *look* almost identical. Even the landscapes in the background show only minor variation, as though all they need to signify is the general idea of 'wilderness' and 'danger'. Verbally, however, there are differences, not only in the voices used, but also in the genres. In the examples above, the 'zoologist' guide uses the genre and language of the 'group leader's announcement', characterised by the imperative, the first person plural and the future tense, in other words by things 'you' *must* do and things 'we' *are going to* do, while the storyteller guide uses the genre and language of the story, with its stock phrases ('once upon a time'), its focus on third person actors and past events, and its concern to provide orientation in time and space.

Following the Aboriginal storyteller, users encounter a kind of scene-setting screen, an establishing shot, to use film language. It is a fairly detailed and realistic picture of an Australian 'Outback' landscape, with a kangaroo at bottom right. At this point written and spoken text begin to diverge:

Written text
Australia is the flattest and driest of all the continents, so much of it is covered by desert. Australia was once connected to other landmasses, but it drifted away from them long ago. Its primitive *marsupials* and *monotremes* were protected by their isolation and were not replaced by animals that evolved later.

Spoken text
(same voice as in the 'Guide Introduction Screen')
In the beginning time, the spirit ancestors of the Aboriginal people lived on earth and they had the characteristics of both animals and people. They dreamed a long dream and in that dreaming the creatures of the earth came to be as we know them now.
The spoken text is followed by intermittent sound effects of distant thunder and crickets.

The written text, indeed the whole 'Australian Outback' screen, is part of the database. The same screen can also be selected by other guides, in other contexts. In the 'Aboriginal Dreamtime Stories' tour it functions as an establishing shot, elsewhere it may be an example of a desert landscape, or a variety of Australian landscape, or the habitat of a particular Australian animal, or a site forming part of the 'Australian Walkabout' tour. The screen forms part of the vast text-resource of the database itself, but that resource can never be observed directly, never be grasped in its own consistency. It remains hidden, buried, and only becomes visible in the form of fragments and snippets which can then be assembled in the various ways foreseen and programmed by the interface designers.

At this point users begin to get some choice, some 'interactivity'. They can ask for definitions of terms highlighted in the written text (terms such as 'marsupial' and 'monotreme'). These definitions are then superimposed on the screen in a box, and the terms themselves are also spoken, by the voice of the guide, now in a different role. Clicking on an icon of the guide, the user encounters a series of screens which provide information about a particular kind of animal. Again, there is both the written text provided by the content providers, and the spoken text provided by the interface designers, the former oriented towards information, the latter oriented towards the guide's 'point of view'.

Here is an example. We have included only one of the three items of written text. Each of the three items has its own picture. Words and pictures are arranged in the way typical of a page in an illustrated encyclopaedia:

Written text
There is a good reason that this Australian snake is called the 'Death Adder'. Before an *antivenin* was developed, half of the people bitten by it died. Luckily, the death adder is not very *aggressive* and bites only if touched.

Spoken text
(in the guide's voice)
In that time there was not yet death. It was the fault of the first humans that death was led into the world (*didgeridoo music starts*). For the moon came

> down to the earth and said to them: 'If you carry my pets across the river you will rise again after you have died and so live forever' (*didgeridoo music fades out*). But the humans refused. They were afraid of the moon's pets which were all deadly snakes. So the moon said: 'Silly humans. Now when you die you will stay dead and I will always send you poisonous snakes to remind you that you disobeyed me.'
> *A loop of intermittent sound effects: birds and frogs; indeterminate rustling.*

After a number of these screens, users are taken to a different type of screen. It not only provides basic information about a topic, but also allows users to 'explore on their own', to branch out into related topics of their choice. The spoken texts of these screens continue the guided tours, but the written texts and pictures differ. They are more eye-catching and dramatic. Instead of clauses like 'The death adder's closest relatives include ...', we have clauses like 'Coiled and ready to strike, a mangrove snake opens its mouth'. Instead of generic reference ('death adders') we have specific reference ('a mangrove snake ...'). Instead of decontextualised descriptive pictures, we see the 'dangerous creatures' in action, and in their habitat. The screen also contains a number of 'hot' captions, in red, which can be clicked to reach other screens ('Salt swamp', 'Tree snakes', 'Odd neighbours', 'Snake or fake?', 'Vicious vine', 'Rear-fanged snakes', and so on). By clicking on these you reach further information screens, and short 'movies'. These further information screens themselves allow further exploration too, but you can only go so far. If you stray too far from the tour, a box appears on the screen:

> Guided tour
> You have made a choice that will lead you away from the guided tour. Do you want to leave the tour now and explore on your own?
> OK CANCEL

In other words, in following the guided tour you first move through a number of information screens of which the order is fixed and in which interactivity is restricted to asking for the definitions of terms. Then, after two, three or four of these, all dealing with the same kind of animal (here the snake), you come to a screen where you can 'explore on your own' (but without straying too far from the tour). If you do come back and follow the guide further, this pattern repeats itself a number of times: you will not only hear stories about snakes, but also about echidnas, spiders, kangaroos, dingoes, platypuses and koalas, until, eventually, the tour closes:

> And so the Dreamtime passed away and the spirit ancestors moved to a mysterious place. But they left us the Earth and its creatures, to love and cherish. This is the end of the voyage into Dreamtime. To go where you will

> click the 'content' button below and explore by yourself. If you want to hear more tales, click my button, to return to the Guide Screen and then choose a new path.

Each of the twelve tours has exactly the same structure. What the interface designer has designed, the 'guided tour', is therefore a fairly rigid genre, a fairly rigid 'assembly format'. As we have seen, the CD-ROM as a whole provides three such 'assembly formats'.

The twelve guided tours all use the *same written text*. As the designers of the original guide interface put it, there is 'a central factual nuggets of names, dates, places, with a constellation of points of view around it' (Oren *et al.*, 1990: 37). This means that we have, in the end, not only generic homogeneity, but also a still deeper, underlying semantic, indeed ideological homogeneity. The problem is that this is not easily visible. Ideology has gone underground. Only snippets and fragments emerge, to be immediately re-assembled and incorporated in the contexts of different guided tours with very different surface ideologies – compare, for instance, Safara's 'Dreamtime stories' to the texts spoken by another guide, Tawny, the female wildlife photographer:

> If you're a female black widow spider you've got it made. You've only got to worry about predators that want to eat you (*laugh*) and most wild animals have to do that. But if you're male you've got to watch out for predators *and* you've also got to worry about the intentions of that female spider you've been seeing. A lot of black widow spiders don't get the chance to kiss and tell because the females eat them after they mate.

But the actual information screens are not affected by these multiple uses. They still say what they say, they still provide an underlying and ultimately coherent 'global' (and 'scientific') meaning system on which the different tours must necessarily feed, and which they must always again make compatible with 'local' meaning systems such as Aboriginal Dreamtime stories or certain kinds of feminist discourses.

Finally, it is important to point out that the interactivity of this CD-ROM does not go beyond 'assembly'. It does not give the user any access to synthesis, to origination, however minor. In the enthusiasm for interactivity, this difference, the difference between giving people 'choice' and giving people control, is sometimes forgotten.

We would like to finish with an example that is more oriented towards 'transmission', a comparison between two websites aimed at women. We draw here on the work of one of our students, Mariana Berutto (1999).

Ivillage was founded in 1995 by Candice Carpenter, a former executive at Time Warner and home shopping channel QVC. It is essentially an online equivalent of the traditional women's magazine. A list of its thirteen channels reads like the table of contents of any women's magazine: Astrology, Better Health, Book Club, Career, Fitness and Beauty, Food, Money/Life, Parent Soup, Parents' Place, Pets, Shopping, Travel, Work from Home. But apart from the familiar information, tips and hints, these channels also provide interactive elements: charts, message boards, and email accounts, as well as, for instance, a mortgage calculator in the Money/Life channel, a calories table in the Fitness and Beauty channel, and so on. In other words, adaptation is mainly oriented towards extending the kind of interactive elements already existing in traditional women's magazines (e.g. letters to ask for advice on a range of matters), just as the advertisements extend the traditional tear-out coupon, making it more immediate and allowing the deal to be closed at once ('e-commerce'). Although it has existed for four years and attracts three million visitors a month, the site still does not make a profit – during the first nine months of 1998 it lost $32 million on revenues of $9 million.

Psycho Men Slayers (PMS) Clan is a totally different kind of website, an online game for women. As documented by Morris (1998), online game playing is almost exclusively oriented towards men. Women players experience a great deal of sexual harassment – name calling, demands for 'net sex', descriptions of their physical attributes, and so on. In some cases female players have been banned from games because the other players did not want women to take part. Accordingly, the 'mission statement' of *PMS* reads as follows:

> PMS was started to allow females to enjoy being part of an online Quake clan, and take part in the fun with their peers who would not reject or laugh at them because they were a girl. From day one, the focus has been on friendship and fun. No matter how good or how bad a girl plays, she 'tries' her very best and she deserves to experience Clan PMS, the friendship and the fun. Clan PMS is a group of females dedicated to bringing female Quake players together.

In games of this kind, the interactive semiotic potential of the internet is used in a way that is entirely different from the previous example. The medium is used, not as a transmission medium, to extend and adapt 'original' forms of interaction such as providing information, offering advice etc., to a larger group of people, but as an originating medium, a medium for creating new forms of interaction. The fifteen women involved in the game do not know each other as they are in 'real life' (it would of course be possible to play the game as a man masquerading as a woman). They (co-)create new personalities and new relationships, a world which only exists on the net. Each member has a page on the site on which she designs a 'virtual' physical description of herself and a name. Some describe themselves as physically strong women carrying big weapons, others as tiny 'angels' or sexy girls. The names, too, are provocative: 'Tank Girl', 'Acid Baby', 'Lady Death', etc. Six members do not reveal their ages, the others say they are in their twenties (but again, there is no reason why they really should be). The site also contains message boards, news sections and a photo album showing photos of members and their children, screen shots from games and a section with pictures of semi-naked men.

The Clan itself has a hierarchical structure, with a clan leader, Aurora, and division leaders. Aspiring members must pass through a recruitment process in which their personality will be evaluated and their skills tested. The recruit then joins a training group to attend practice sessions, meetings and so on. If she turns out to be a good team player, she will eventually be invited to become a full member, and pledge allegiance to a code of conduct. Those who do not follow the code are moved to an 'inactive list' and will not be allowed to play for a period of time. A site of this kind combines representation (drama) and interaction (game) in a novel way: it represents/dramatises/enacts desires, themes and ideas which, in themselves, are familiar from contemporary mass media mythology, but are realised here in an entirely novel way. We believe these games should not be seen in terms of 'realism', as if players can no longer tell the difference between 'real' and 'virtual' reality and have lost all touch with embodiment as they wander through a cyber-world, but as a new, and newly (inter)active form of representation. Outsiders can laugh at the crudity of the characters and the plots. They would probably have laughed also at the crudity of the earliest movies, with their stock characters and 'chase' plots. The importance of these games does not lie in their old content but in the new mode of participating in society's narratives which they introduce, the same type of participation mode we also described in relation to music: a move away from decontextualised representation and imaginary identification towards participation, community and co-creation. Games may yet become a key art form of the twenty-first century.

6 Issues for the multimodal agenda

A multimodal theory of communication

In this chapter we will review what it is we think we have done, pointing up some things more sharply, and also drawing attention to some of the things which we have not done here, some of the things we would like to put on the multimodal agenda.

So what have we done? First and foremost we have tried to show that meaning is made in many different ways, always, in the many different modes and media which are co-present in a communicational ensemble. This entails that a past (and still existent) common sense to the effect that meaning resides in language alone – or, in other versions of this, that language is the central means of representing and communicating even though there are 'extra-linguistic', 'para-linguistic' things going on as well – is simply no longer tenable, that it never really was, and certainly is not now.

In trying to demonstrate the characteristics of these multimodal ensembles we have sketched a multimodal theory of communication which concentrates on two things: (1) the *semiotic resources* of communication, the modes and the media used, and (2) the communicative practices in which these resources are used. These communicative practices are seen as multi-layered and include, at the very least, discursive practices, production practices and interpretive practices, while they may also include design practices and/or distribution practices. We have stressed that each of these layers contributes to meaning. The key point here is that meaning is made not only with a multiplicity of semiotic resources, in a multiplicity of modes and media, but also at different 'places' within each of these. As we have pointed out, linguists have taken language to be unique because on the one hand it has realisational resources which do not make a contribution to meaning (form, both as phonology and as grammar/syntax) and on the other hand it has meaning resources which can be used to express the meanings of the individual users of the resources. By contrast, we assume that meaning is made everywhere, in every 'layer', in phonology and in grammar/syntax. In any one mode *all* realisational elements are available for the making of signs, and are used for that. From the moment that a culture has made the decision to draw a particular material into its communicative processes, that material has become part of the cultural and semiotic resources of that culture and is available for use in the making of signs.

Theoretically this means that 'double articulation' (the single, once-and-for-all expression of meaning in form) is not and cannot be a feature of multimodal representation and communication. In every mode of the multimodal ensemble there is always 'work' with all the available representational forms, and such work is always meaningful.

Semiotic resources

Semiotic resources have been produced in the course of social/cultural/political histories – histories which of course keep on going. New social, cultural and political needs lead to new ways of communicating and to new communication technologies – as well as to new communication theories. In Chapter 5 we saw how the 1920s required new forms of public communication as the suburban family home increasingly became the focus of social life. Radio, which had existed as a two-way medium with limited uses for some thirty years, turned into broadcasting, and powerful institutions such as the BBC were founded everywhere. The same period also saw a new interest in voice and intonation on the part of linguists. It became important to produce explicit knowledge about this mode which previously had been left to its own devices. But as is often the case, knowledge and power were closely related. The BBC formed a pronunciation committee whose inaugural members included both George Bernard Shaw and the phonetician Daniel Jones. Reithian radio was not only to raise the cultural level of the nation, it was also to spread 'proper' English speech and do away with inferior dialects. Today similar movements are beginning in relation to visual communication, though now steered by multinational corporations and software developers, rather than by state broadcasting and education systems.

Semiotic resources exist in different ways for different people and groups. The English language, as a resource, provides hundreds of thousands of words, but only language specialists use more than 18,000 of them and most people get by with 6,000–7,000. Many semiotic resources are reserved for specialists, or known in different ways by those who actively use them for semiotic production and those who are their 'receivers' ('consumers', 'users', etc.). In many areas of semiotic production, the gap between producers and consumers continues to widen, for instance in the production of food and dress.

Semiotic resources may take the form of more or less loose collections of signs or the form of systems of rules – or something in between. Books such as the *Dictionary of Visual Language* (Thompson and Davenport, 1982) provide an alphabetically ordered list of individual icons and design ideas, each with a short gloss on its meaning-potential and on the way it has been used by selected key designers. Such books are lexicons, more or less unordered storehouses of ideas and resources where you can browse, 'shop' for ideas in the same way as you can shop for your shoes or shirts in a store. Grammars, on the other hand, use very broad, abstract classes of items, but provide fairly definite rules for combining them into an infinite number of possible utterances. They are decontextualised and abstract, but also powerful in what can be done with them. Perhaps it is no wonder that grammatically organised modes have tended to be the most powerful modes (or the province of the powerful specialists who monopolise the knowledge and know-how of design and production in specific modes).

No semiotic resource is by 'nature' either 'lexically' or 'grammatically' organised. Interestingly, as language loses some of its power, theories of language are becoming more 'lexical' and less 'grammatical'. More and more linguists, particularly in areas such as corpus linguistics and 'formulaic language', now conceive of people's knowledge of language not in the way Chomsky did, as a small, economical set of rules that can generate an infinite number of linguistic utterances, but as a vast, maze-like storehouse of words and collocations of words, of fragments of language, idioms etc.: in short, in the way in which people used to conceive of the visual mode. At the same time, the first visual grammars are appearing – our own work has been part of this move (Kress and Van Leeuwen, 1996). Construction toys for children are another example of increasing 'lexicalisation'. Toys such as Lego used to provide a limited number of highly abstract building blocks with which very many different objects could be made, whereas now they tend towards providing a large number of ready-made objects that can be assembled into scenes.

Once a mode has begun to become 'grammaticalised', it will acquire some other powerful and highly valued facilities, such as the ability to produce meta-signs, to comment on representations in that same mode, and to produce theoretical statements. In the case of the visual, the postmodern stress on visual irony, pastiche, parody etc. can be seen as a forerunner of visual meta-language. Computer interfaces now develop it further. As for the possibility of visual theoretical statements, in science the process of computer-aided visual modelling is already well advanced, and we might add that art has often pre-figured this, in the way that the paintings of Malevitch, for instance, prefigured/anticipated the pixels of the computer screen, or the geometrical paintings of the De Stijl group prefigured their later interior designs and architectural designs.

Finally, it is possible that a mode is 'grammatical' to some of its users, and 'lexical' to others, especially in cases where there is a gap between producers and consumers, and where the producer's knowledge of design and production is kept more or less secret. For most people 'smell' is a collection of distinct individual smells, often associated with specific, individual memories, and evaluated in highly subjective ways. But for the scientists, perfumers, aromatherapists etc. who produce smells, there are systems. Aromatherapists recognise about fifty basic smells, which can combine into a much larger number of complex smells by means of a syntax of 'head', 'body' and 'base' in which each of the three components of the complex smell-sign must have specific characteristics, for instance in terms of degree of volatility. These complex smells, finally, can be combined into an indefinite number of specific aromas.

In other words, what to the consumer is a collection of individual specific experiences, is to the producer, in this case, a rule-governed system, structured in some ways not entirely unlike language, with the number of basic smells being of the same order as the number of phonemes in languages. In our approach, an either/or distinction between smells as unique and individual and smell as a rule-governed system is a false one. The two dimensions, the two kinds of meaning, are both always present – produced in different layers of the semiotic resources used, and through different aspects of the communicative practices in which they are used.

Communicative practice

Communicative practices always involve both representation and interaction. First of all, by communicating we *interact*, we do something to or for or with people – entertain them with stories, persuade them to do or think something, debate issues with them, tell them what to do, and so on. None of these communicative activities can exist without being linked to some form of representational 'content', not only in language, but also in all other modes (for the argument about music, which is often said to have no content, see Van Leeuwen, 1999). In our approach we have conceived of representational content also in terms of social practice. We have defined discourse as a knowledge which is (1) a knowledge of practices, of how things are or must be done (at the level of discourse these two merge), together with specific evaluations and legitimations of and purposes for these practices, and (2) a knowledge which is linked to and activated in the context of specific communicative practices. This means that people may at different times draw on different discourses about the same practice or practices, choosing the one they see as most adequate to their own interests in the given context. In Chapter 2 we discussed family dinner discourses first of all in terms of 'who eats what with whom, where, when, with what implements' and so on, in other words, in terms of a particular family dinner *scenario*, and second, in terms of a set of evaluations, legitimations and purposes that habitually or conventionally go with that scenario. In the example they were expressed through the colour *blue*, whose meaning was anchored both by visual references to sky and sea and by verbal references to evaluative qualities ('serene, yet dynamic').

The point is that a given discourse cannot only be realised by a range of semiotic resources (colour, words, pictures, in a television programme perhaps 'serene, yet dynamic' music), it can also be inserted into a range of communicative practices. It can, for instance, be inserted into a conversation between a husband and wife about how to remodel their kitchen, or in a home magazine feature. But it cannot be inserted into just any context. In Chapter 1, for instance, we saw that English magazines and the Swedish IKEA catalogue used different scenarios of 'who does what with whom' in children's bedrooms. In Chapter 2 we saw that English and French magazines attach different evaluations to kitchens and dining rooms. There can also be a difference between how families or magazines talk about the family dinner and what (specific) families actually do. A representation of the family dinner is not the family dinner itself. Things will be left out, changed, and added (the key additions are of course the evaluations, legitimations and purposes). Again, what will be changed, left out or added will differ according to the interests of the communicative practice into which the discourse is inserted. We have dealt with this in greater detail elsewhere (e.g. Van Leeuwen, 1993; Van Leeuwen and Wodak, 1999). Here we will use a further, short example, to show how the same text can be analysed twice, once as discursive practice, and once as interactive practice or 'design'. The first text comes from a magazine advertisement for a baby toy in the shape of a large pillow with a piano painted on it. There are five sections in the shape of piano keys, and pressing on them produces five different noises. Figure 6.1 shows the layout of the advertisement. The headline on top (1) says, 'It's a great age to kick a few tunes around!'. Below (2) we see a smiling baby kicking the toy. The inset photo (3) shows another, somewhat older baby playing the 'piano' with his or her hands. The text below the main picture (4) introduces the 'kick 'n' play piano' and addresses baby directly: 'Get down to some foot-tappin' music, animal sounds and twinkly lights at the bottom of your cot ... then, when you can get your hands on that keyboard, take the floor and play!' Finally (5) there is an indication of the age range of the toy ('birth and up'), the price, and the number of a customer careline. The second text comes from the parenting magazine *New Baby* (Fig. 6.2). Figure 6.2 shows a whole page, but the section on which we will concentrate in particular, 'Mobiles and baby gyms', runs as follows:

> Mobiles and baby gyms
> Cot mobiles and gyms are great for very small babies because they give them something to look at, particularly if they have toys that move round when the mechanism is wound up, or have twinkling lights. They're great for teaching hand–eye coordination, and cause and effect – if your baby bats the hanging toys with his hands or feet, they'll move and maybe make a noise. Show your baby how to swipe things, then let him explore. Many baby gyms have activities on the sides as well as the top, to encourage your baby to roll over.

Both texts are about 'what mothers and babies do with cot toys'. They are therefore very similar in terms of discourse. But they are by no means identical. In the parenting magazine, the scenario, the underlying sequence of events, is more or less as follows (leaving off the final clause):

Figure 6.1 *Layout of advertisement for 'kick 'n' play piano'*

1. Very small babies look at toys-that-move-around-and-have-twinkling-lights [evaluation: 'great'].
2. Mothers shows babies how to swipe things [purpose: teaching hand–eye coordination].
3. Mothers let babies explore.
4. Babies 'bat at' the hanging toys to make them move and produce a noise.

In the advertisement the scenario is as follows:

1. Babies tap with their feet on pianos, thus producing music, animal sounds and twinkling lights [evaluation: fun].

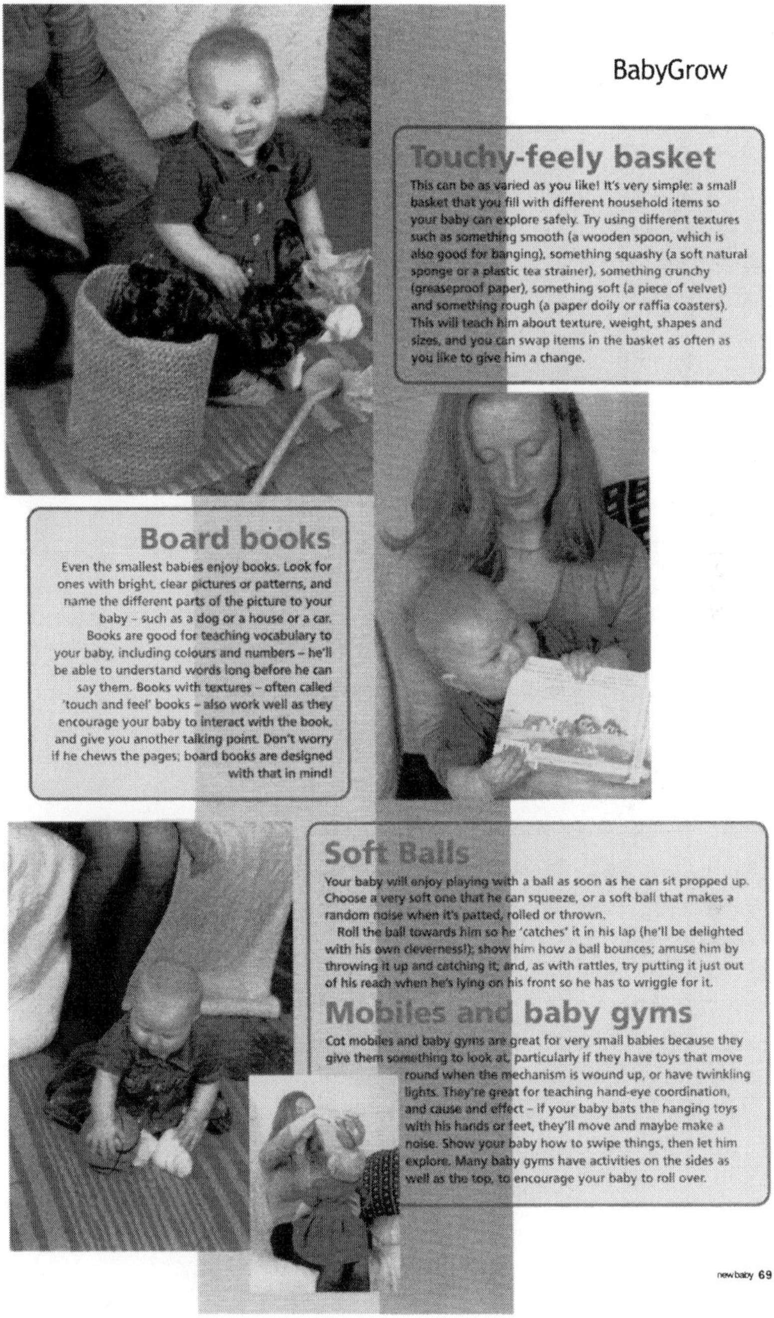

BabyGrow

Touchy-feely basket

This can be as varied as you like! It's very simple: a small basket that you fill with different household items so your baby can explore safely. Try using different textures such as something smooth (a wooden spoon, which is also good for banging), something squashy (a soft natural sponge or a plastic tea strainer), something crunchy (greaseproof paper), something soft (a piece of velvet) and something rough (a paper doily or raffia coasters). This will teach him about texture, weight, shapes and sizes, and you can swap items in the basket as often as you like to give him a change.

Board books

Even the smallest babies enjoy books. Look for ones with bright, clear pictures or patterns, and name the different parts of the picture to your baby – such as a dog or a house or a car. Books are good for teaching vocabulary to your baby, including colours and numbers – he'll be able to understand words long before he can say them. Books with textures – often called 'touch and feel' books – also work well as they encourage your baby to interact with the book, and give you another talking point. Don't worry if he chews the pages; board books are designed with that in mind!

Soft Balls

Your baby will enjoy playing with a ball as soon as he can sit propped up. Choose a very soft one that he can squeeze, or a soft ball that makes a random noise when it's patted, rolled or thrown.

Roll the ball towards him so he 'catches' it in his lap (he'll be delighted with his own cleverness!); show him how a ball bounces; amuse him by throwing it up and catching it; and, as with rattles, try putting it just out of his reach when he's lying on his front so he has to wriggle for it.

Mobiles and baby gyms

Cot mobiles and baby gyms are great for very small babies because they give them something to look at, particularly if they have toys that move round when the mechanism is wound up, or have twinkling lights. They're great for teaching hand-eye coordination, and cause and effect – if your baby bats the hanging toys with his hands or feet, they'll move and maybe make a noise. Show your baby how to swipe things, then let him explore. Many baby gyms have activities on the sides as well as the top, to encourage your baby to roll over.

newbaby 69

Figure 6.2 *Double page spread from* New Baby *(May 2000)*

2. Babies get their hands on keyboards and play (timing: when they are ready for it) [evaluation: fun].

So the two discourses differ in a number of ways. First, in the parenting magazine, mothers play a role, whereas in the advertisement they do not. Second, in the parenting text the babies progress from looking to doing, whereas in the advertisement this is not the case – the baby depicted is not even looking at what s/he is doing. Third, in the parenting text the 'educational' purpose of the toys is explicitly formulated, whereas the advertisement only emphasises 'fun' (through the colours and the smile, as we will later discuss more fully) and construes the child not as a baby but already in terms of 'young adult' activity, through the allusions to rock 'n' roll (kick 'n' play) and the design of the instrument (other toys producing noise may not be shaped like a recognisable musical instrument). In other words, here a baby is seen practising at being a rock star, rather than at universal Piagetian skills, and as being in the social world already.

In other words, the scenario of babies' play is differently constructed and differently provided with values and purposes in the two discourses. A study of more of these texts would reveal to which degree these discourses underlie other parenting texts and advertisements as well (we think they do). More importantly, the discourses are the way they are because of the interests that prevail in the context. The advertisement must sell and does so by emphasising the affective satisfaction the product will provide; the parenting text must provide serious advice and emphasise educational purposes and psychological legitimations, with pleasure at best as a means to an end rather than an end in itself.

The key point, however, is that discourse is here itself seen as a (recontextualisation of) social practice. Clearly some texts will recontextualise a lot of the actual activities that are part of the practice and add relatively few evaluations, purposes and legitimations, at least at an explicit level (e.g. narratives), while others will provide scant and more generalised reference to the activities of the practices and concentrate on the construction of evaluations, legitimation (or critiques) and purposes (e.g. theoretical arguments). But that does not change the fact that discourse is always grounded in social practice, in what we do, and that without such grounding, meaning would not be possible.

Design

The discourses we have just described can be realised in many different modes and inserted in many different communicative practices – all of which will add layers of meaning to them. The discourse of the mother playing with her baby, for instance, could also be drawn on for an episode in a story, which would take away its explicit function of providing parental advice (of course stories can also be read as models for life), and that story could be told orally, written, be on film, and so on, with all the differences in the selection of semiotic resources which that involves. Again, the discourse underlying the advertisement could also be drawn on in a conversation between two mothers, and then it would perhaps follow the schema which, as Labov (1972) has shown, underlies the way people tell each other of their experiences in conversation, starting with an 'abstract' ('listen what my baby did the other day'), then providing some background ('well you know that piano I bought for her'), and an initial situation ('so far she's only been kicking at it'), a development ('but yesterday I was just sitting there, reading a magazine, and suddenly I heard her play differently, and then, you know, I looked around and there she was, playing it with her hands'), an 'evaluation' ('isn't that amazing') and a 'coda' ('I bet she's going to be a star'). The main difference between such a scenario and a recontextualised one is that this one is actually enacted, rather than represented, and that means that we cannot directly observe the evaluations, legitimations and purposes of the communicative act – that is, we cannot directly observe what the two women think of telling stories of this kind, what they see as its purpose and so on; we can only observe the concrete elements of who says what to whom, how, where, when etc.

Design, whether it actually leads to a physical 'sketch', 'blueprint', or 'score', or only exists (or is thought up) as a schema-for-production in the mind, adds two things to the discourse: (1) it contextualises, makes it work within the context of a communicative interaction (such as 'giving parental advice', 'telling a story', 'advertising a product') by, creatively or otherwise, drawing on semiotic resources such as generic schemas for stories, advertisements etc.; and (2) it selects which modes will be used to realise which aspects of that communicative interaction, whether by drawing on conventions such as the visual depiction of the satisfaction of the product in full-page magazine advertisements or not. The parenting text (Fig. 6.2), for instance, does not visually depict the section on mobiles and baby gyms; but it does show babies whose facial expressions signify concentration, focusing on a learning task, rather than experiencing pleasure, as in the advertisement. It has designed the article as a fairly loose collection of 'bits of information', examples of things you can do with your child, rather than as a text with a beginning, a middle and an end. Looking now at the section on mobiles and baby gyms, the new scenario, the scenario of 'giving parental advice' (rather than 'playing with baby'), goes more or less as follows:

1. [Author] states the value [of cot mobiles and baby gyms] and gives two reasons for doing so.
2. [Author] advises [the parent to show baby how to swipe, and to then let her explore].

Clearly both the overall spatial schema of the double page, with its 'bits of information' and this little sequential schema, could also be used in connection with other discourses, if we replace the bracketed representational content with other content. Equally clearly, both could also have been expressed through different media, e.g. through television or a website. This, too, is part of 'design', in the sense in which we use the term here: to select the chosen modes and media, and the ways in which the various communicative acts involved (providing 'bits of information', 'authoritatively stating the value of something', 'advising people to take a certain course of action') will be signified in these various modes, whether singly or in combination.

As for the advertisement (Fig. 6.1), we can enumerate the communicative acts, but there is no guarantee that they will be read in this order, because the text is spatially rather than sequentially organised:

1. Providing memorable catchphrase (slogan on top).
2. Showing the satisfaction of using the product in one way (the large picture).
3. Announcing the product itself (headline of copy, underneath the large picture).
4. Telling the consumer (the baby, ostensibly!) to use the product (copy).
5. Showing the satisfaction of another (later) use of the product (second picture).
6. Stating age range.
7. Stating price.
8. Providing 'careline' telephone number.

Here, spatial order – where the elements are placed, how salient they are made, and in which ways they are visually framed off from each other or connected to each other, e.g. by superimposition, colour harmony etc. – becomes the key aspect of the design schema, not sequential order, which is left to the reader, or, at best, suggested by hierarchies of salience. Clearly the photo of the baby playing piano with its feet is not only central and most salient, it is also most crucial in conveying the action itself (playing the piano with the feet), and its values/satisfactions (the vibrant red, oranges and yellows, the smile on the baby's face). The schemas are layout schemas and colour schemas (the colours of the scene rhyme with those of the product itself), a schema which is applied not only in other advertisements, but also, for instance, in home magazines (see the discussion of blue and white in *Maison Française* in Chapters 2 and 3).

Design thus inserts a discourse, a habitual or conventional way of thinking/talking about what small babies do, into a communicative interaction. But that communicative interaction itself is not fully specified by a description of the 'text'. The text gives us only the activities, the 'what' ('state the value', 'advise'), and the 'how' (which modes how deployed), and not the other elements shared by all practices – the 'who', 'where', 'when', 'with what'. A full description of communicative practices must also involve these elements – and in cases such as advertising where there is a gap between the place and time of production and interpretation, that involves both the who, what, where, when of production and the who, what, where, when of interpretation.

Production and distribution

All of this still does not touch on how the design will actually be produced. Because they are relatively abstract, design schemas such as we have just discussed can be produced in many different ways, which leaves much room for creativity, for 'production' thinking. Take for instance the schema of 'separate bits of information' in Figure 6.2. The *way* in which it is produced, with boxes distributed across the pages, adds further meaning. In the past, boxes of this kind were usually smaller in number and inserted in a conventionally laid-out article, providing the graphic equivalent of the footnote, the expansion of a detail, but they are now used in a much more prominent way, indeed sometimes more prominent than the text itself. Here we have *only* such footnotes. Information has become a series of separate items, at best connected by a common theme. The shape of the boxes is also relevant here – rather than the shape of a box, it is the shape of a television or computer frame. Print now takes its cue from the visual media, rather than the other way around.

The point of this explanation is not whether we are right or not. The point is that we have used the principles of provenance and experiential metaphor to create an interpretation. We have used some arguments based on 'where such frames have been', on their cultural history, and some arguments based on 'what they literally are': separate, strongly framed off from each other, etc. In thc absence of a 'grammar' to help us along, we have used, to put it another way, modes of interpretation oriented towards 'cultural studies' and 'phenomenology'. And we assume that the producers did so as well, whether intentionally or not. It may be that a new design language will develop (or be built into software) which will be much more prescriptive of what various types of boxes express and when you should or should not use them. In that case 'production thinking' will have transformed into or merged with 'design thinking'. But there are equally many signs of a renewed interest in 'production thinking', and in the materialities of communicative interaction in all its forms.

The same line of reasoning can be followed with respect to the use of a 'handwriting' font in the advertisement. To interpret 'handwriting' as a sign here, we need to think about where handwriting has been and is, and this, increasingly, is in the realm of the 'personal message'. This use of 'handwriting' as a sign of personal address has already become conventional, but that does not mean that it has 'grammaticalised', as has personal and impersonal address in language, through the pronoun system for instance. Typography is still 'lexical', it still works through connotation (not least because it has been thought about as arbitrary, only concerned with 'readability'), and 'handwriting' as sign is still part of that lexicon of design ideas we talked about. That this semiotic resource should be used a great deal in advertising should not surprise us: advertising often seeks to address its audiences as unique individuals, rather than as the groups of people with conforming consumption patterns which they really are.

The technological form – in this case that of the printed magazine – is not only important because it allows the message to be preserved and mass distributed. The paper used, for instance, conveys the almost ineffable but very important meanings of *gloss*. Compare an advertisement in a glossy magazine to its colour photocopy or computer printout and the difference becomes immediately apparent. A crucial element of the magazine's seductive power is lost. And the material qualities of the magazine also contribute *interactive* meanings. Just as there is an enormous difference between being immersed in a movie in the cinema and zapping from television channel to channel, so there is an enormous difference between reading a book from cover to cover and leafing through a magazine. The weight and size of the magazine allow it to be carried to different places; the way it is bound and the quality of the paper allow it to be leafed through, cut out from, and so on. Such interactive aspects, realised in the material and kinetic qualities of the object itself, are of increasing significance in the age of 'interactivity'.

Semiotic stratification and social stratification

Throughout this book we have stressed that discourse, design, production and distribution are not abstract semiotic layers. They represent practices which can aggregate and disaggregate in different ways. When 'kinds of doings' in professions or other workplaces change, for instance, so will 'kinds of doing' in semiotic terms. Again this shows clearly that we cannot be absolute about what constitutes a semiotic practice, or a design, or a mode, because all these are the effects of work in changing social circumstances. Of course we are aware that our insight in this respect does not come out of the blue, so to speak, but rather is an insight made possible precisely by the present social, political, cultural and economic circumstances, where one cannot but notice such aggregations and disaggregations. We have pointed to these in relation to a number of examples: teaching in schools, and increasingly now also in universities in Anglophone countries around the world; film-production; journalism; multimedia production. We pointed out that the change is not all in one direction. In some instances there has been aggregation, as in journalism and in multimedia production where formerly distinct practices – social, professional, and semiotic – have been brought together into a new aggregation, performed by one individual.

In Britain this has more recently also extended to the National Health Service, where the traditional demarcation lines between the roles of nurse, general practitioner, consultant and so on have been blurred very radically. In other instances there has been disaggregation, as in teaching in England for instance, where a complex of practices formerly all resting with one individual have been disaggregated and fewer of these left with one individual; or as in certain instances of book-'authoring', such as textbook-'authoring', where formerly one single 'author' was responsible for the 'writing' of the book, a task now taken over by a team. In other words, the movements might be seen as nearly contradictory. Some professions are being or becoming deskilled, while new practices (usually too new to be professionalised) are bringing together a multiplicity of formerly discrete skills.

We need in each case to look at the environment in which the practice has its place; it is not the case that technology alone is responsible. In some cases technology plays no part at all. In the case of multimedia production technology is the issue. The possibilities of the representation of a variety of distinct semiotic modes in the one digitised, electronic form (whether sound in its various modal aspects, or image, or word) and providing a technological means of production which at that one level need not distinguish between modal articulation, makes the previously technically, materially and professionally distinct forms of production come together through and in the affordances of the new technology. In the case of teaching, by contrast, technology is not the issue: here the issue is that of (political) control of an ever more contentious area. Of course, this particular instance of disaggregation can be linked to matters of technology quite easily if we wish to do so: we can say that education will need to make more and more use of the new technologies for reasons of efficiency and cost. And in this new regime we cannot have teachers function as they did in the former regime. It is important at points like these to be able to tell apart the actual causes and motivations for aggregations and disaggregations from ideologically motivated ones: not only for (the ultimately more important) political reasons, that is, so as not to be hoodwinked by seemingly plausible arguments, but also for semiotic/theoretical reasons; after all we cannot hope to produce semiotically plausible responses to situations which are fundamentally misrepresented. Political arguments need political responses; semiotic arguments need semiotic ones.

In the case of certain contemporary forms of book-'authoring', the disaggregations are not so obviously 'political' as they are in the case of teaching: contemporary textbooks are the products of 'teams', headed usually not by the 'author' in the traditional sense, but by the designer. This shows an important facet of multimodal representation and communication, which we spoke about in the chapter on design practices, Chapter 3. Of course, some of the reasons for the move towards the more intensely multimodal form of text are 'political', that is, they have to do with questions of power and knowledge. In the case of the science textbook the issue is one of the kind of audience which the textbook is attempting to address, and in what form that is to be done. The motives for posing that question are political: the effects of it on the shapings of knowledge have far-reaching cultural, social and political consequences.

The relation between social (and professional) practices and corresponding semiotic practices is a crucial one in our approach, because it demonstrates the entire connectedness of the more directly semiotic aspects of representation and communication and the seemingly less directly semiotic environmental aspects. It also opens the door, at least potentially, to an answer to the question: why the move to a much greater degree of multimodality? (Or, why the move from the seemingly monomodal to the clearly multimodal communicational landscape?) Or why, at the very least, a move towards the recognition of the always present multimodality of communication, now? Multimodality is not a new phenomenon by any means but is, if our account is plausible, a feature of social semiosis always. So why the interest now?

Our approach makes it plausible to attempt to 'read' the social from the semiotic: not in the sense of an unproblematic reading-off of the social from the semiotic, but in the sense that there is a plausibility in attempts to do so. When, in the early seventeenth century, the Counter-Reformation in Europe began its attack on Protestantism, it did so in a variety of ways, not least in the field of the aesthetic. Those who had initially been wooed away from the excesses of Roman Catholicism by the austerity of the new Protestant faiths and of their places of worship, might now be won back (or those who might have been wavering might be convinced to stay) by the exuberant, multi-sensorial appeal of the new churches of that era. The churches of the high baroque in southern parts of Europe make an appeal to the senses, not to reason; to the body, not to the mind. The differences of a theological/ideological kind between Catholicism and Protestantism are realised in the modes of representation, which acted to communicate that message powerfully.

What have we not done?

One thing which we have – most obviously – not done is to produce more grammars of modes other than language. We ourselves have made attempts in that direction in the case of a grammar of images (Kress and Van Leeuwen, 1996) and in the case of grammars of modes utilising the materiality of sound (Van Leeuwen, 1999). Others have made similar moves, for instance in relation to image (O'Toole, 1994), and to action, as we have mentioned earlier (Martinec, 1996; also Kress *et al.*, 2000). But that has not been our intention here. In many instances we have suggested where such grammars might be appropriate and necessary. For us there is also now a slight question about the fundamental issue of whether grammars of distinct modes are quite so uncontentiously 'there' as our own efforts in relation to images, for instance, suggest. We mentioned just above that the question of what a mode is is to be decided in relation to specific instances, to specific (historical) times, to specific groups. For an aromatherapist there is a 'grammar' of smell; for a novelist who uses (descriptions of) smell as a resource for evoking moods and atmospheres there is not. Or, to take another example, for us it is apparent that paper comes in very different forms, colours, weight, texture, etc., all of which constitute resources for making meaning; but we are not sufficiently part of a community which treats (types of) paper as a mode, and as authors we cannot choose on what kind of paper our work will be printed and hence what meanings paper will add to our work.

'Language' is a good case in point: is it best to think of 'language' as a mode, or to think of speech as a mode, and of writing as a mode? And if we chose the latter route, what is it in the mode of speech that unites, in terms of materiality, the pitch variation of intonation with the sequencings of syntax as one kind of materiality? How are lexis and syntax to be thought of as 'the same' in terms of materiality? That constitutes one kind of question. Others have to do with a related issue: if the boundaries around modes are relatively permeable so that the question 'what is part of the mode and what is not' is not easily decided, and if then phenomena which we might have thought of as unquestionably constituting one mode are beginning to look like multimodal ensembles, then maybe the attempt to describe 'grammars' of modes *as such* may not be the best way to proceed.

We seem to be at an odd moment in history, when frames are dissolving everywhere, and formerly clear boundaries are becoming ever more blurred. It is not therefore surprising that the same may be happening with representational resources. We may be approaching a time when the question is not so much 'what discrete modes are occurring together?' as 'what ensembles of resources are being produced?'. Writing, for instance, is freeing itself from its previously seemingly fixed appearance on the page: in a line, followed by other lines, moving in direction from left to right, down the page. As is already the case with some writing systems based on characters (Chinese in Hong Kong, Japanese in Japan), directionality is now a variable, a matter of choice, in many genres, and as such it is a means for making meaning, along with many other features of those script systems.

We have not explored the crucial issue of 'affordances' in any detail; we have raised it here and there, but we have not given much space to any detailed discussion of it. In our account there is a degree of vagueness about this matter. Is affordance more to do with the materiality of the medium in which the mode is constituted, or is it more a matter of the work of a particular culture with a medium over time, or is it a combination of both, sometimes more the one, sometimes more the other? It is a question which is in need of more exploration.

In the case of sign-languages, so called (American Sign Language, British Sign Language), we have a multimodal ensemble, drawing on the different material resources of movement – of the limbs of the upper torso, of facial expression, rhythmic features, etc. Clearly, signing is very closely related to gesture, as in its everyday use in communities who use speech. Is one to be treated as a mode and the other not? In the case of gesture, we might think that it has certain limitations as a means for meaning-making, and that it is therefore rightly always assigned to a secondary role in relation to language. Yet when one community invests 'work' over extended time in that potential then it readily becomes a full representational and communicational resource, a mode. The difference lies, it seems obvious, not in limitations of the material resource, but in the relative degree of work invested over time by the community that uses gesture for purposes of communication. Where speech has been available as a means for representation, gesture *has* remained less developed; where it was not, it has been articulated into a full means for representation. And 'gesture' can stand in here as a representative case for many other instances.

But that is one aspect only. The other has to do with the question: what can a mode do (well) and what can it not do (well)? Here we would need to investigate issues such as what kinds of signs are made in the spatial mode of image as compared to the temporal mode of speech; and to speculate perhaps on what signs are less likely to be made in one or the other; and even to ask if certain signs are impossible in one, and possible in the other. Certainly it is possible to see real differences between the modes of speech on the one hand and of image on the other (leaving writing out of the argument here for the moment because of its complicating spatial aspects). If in a science lesson there is a discussion of, let us say, the characteristic structures of a plant cell, then in a spoken (and also in a written) representation we might say: 'A plant cell consists of a cell-wall, a nucleus, some chloroplasts ...'. In such a representation no commitment is asked or made about a question which in an account in the visual mode is unavoidable, namely about the (spatial) placement and relation of these elements in relation to each other. In a drawing of the cell the nucleus simply has to be placed somewhere: whether in the centre, or more to the side, or wherever. But it has to be positioned *somewhere.* But the moment that positioning is made, a commitment has been made that it is *this place here* and not another where the nucleus *is* located. In a verbal account – spoken or written – that question does not arise as a consequence of the use of the mode: it can be raised, but it need not be.

In explorations of this kind we are then drawn into complex questions at the level of theory and of practice – not to mention 'reality'. How can we hope to untangle the work of culture, often over very long spans of time, from the givens of nature which appear both in the material stuff of modes and in the physiology of bodies perceiving and representing with modes? Of course, the limitations imposed by nature can be 'worked against': that which is by nature spatial can in culture be made (more) temporal, and vice versa. The structures of narrative develop from the sequential nature of speech; but the often enormously complex structures of actual narratives – whether of interpolations, flash-backs, repetitions – are ways of producing artefacts of a quasi-spatial kind; just as certain sound-installations work to produce three-dimensional spatial effects. And we know that space can be used as a medium/mode for narrative: whether in the narratives of hunts or battles scratched or painted on rock-walls or ceilings of caves millennia ago; or the triumphal columns of emperors or kings; or the Bayeux tapestry; or contemporary film.

But beyond that lie the givens of nature in the form of the human body and its sensory engagement with the world: the sense of sight gives access to the world differently from the sense of hearing, the senses of touch, smell, taste. The modes which derive from the materiality of the world lead to differential engagement by the body. The relations of speech through hearing, image through sight are clear enough. But writing, as we mentioned just above, is complex: it is graphic and spatial, yet in many of its characteristics it leans on the forms of speech in many ways (even if heavily modified in cultures with longer histories of (alphabetic) writing), above all in its uses of the basic syntactic/semantic/informational unit of the clause. As we have shown at various points in the preceding chapters, modes develop a secondary materiality which moves away from the immediate materiality of the physical world and of the direct unmediated sensory engagement of the body. In the case of writing it seems that we have such an instance: the secondary materiality of the arrangements of speech are represented in the material mode of the graphic aspects of writing, making writing a composite mode, so to speak.

In the move into a more insistently, intensely multimodal world, such questions become central: they find their reflections in the jeremiads in newspapers, pronouncements by politicians, media pundits and academic commentators alike, about declining 'standards' in literacy and the collapse of the culture treasured by them. Such comments point both to a recognition of a deep change in the representational world, and to an inability to understand it other than in terms of a common sense – theoretical or popular – formed in that past, formed in the era dominated by theories of monomodality. Whether in relation to schooling, or in relation to the newer forms of the economy, there are questions here about forms of cognition, possibilities for learning, new shapings of knowledge, the management of information, and the shaping of forms of human subjectivity different from those around which current understandings are formed.

Some further questions

To some extent these questions surface regularly over longer stretches of time, even if therefore in different contexts. The questions about cognition, learning, knowledge, subjectivity, for instance, are in some ways a replay of those that cluster around the so-called Sapir–Whorf hypothesis. It stated that our understandings of the world are derived from the categories 'given to us' by 'our' language. That argument has remained inconclusive: in its strong form – that we cannot see, perceive, think outside of the categories provided by language – it seems untenable. Patently enough, we can; though we need to work harder to do so. In its weak form – that the categories of language provide grooves for habituated thought – it seems difficult to escape. The fact that the argument has remained inconclusive does not mean that it is unimportant, even though critics of the hypothesis have used that fact to dismiss it as trivial or silly.

Here we will briefly explore just two topics around these questions: the shapes of narrative in different modal configurations, and the question of 'control'. First, then, narrative: how is narrative shaped in a specific mode, and how is it reshaped when it appears in different modes? We start by recounting rather than fully representing here (this and other examples which pertain to this issue can be found in Kress *et al.*, 2000) one example from a science classroom: it concerns the representation in verbal and visual form of the topic 'blood circulation'. This had been discussed over a series of four lessons. At the conclusion of the series, the students had been asked to undertake two different tasks: one, done as work in class, was the construction of 'concept maps', and the other, done as homework, was the writing of a 'story' describing the life of a red blood cell in its journey around the body (Fig. 6.3). 'Concept maps' required the arrangement in a spatial display of a number (about thirty in this case) of small cards, each of which had a 'concept' written on it (Fig. 6.4). The 'maps' produced represented the student's sense of the relation between the elements/concepts involved.

A common discourse about an aspect of the body was thus given, but the students were given a certain amount of freedom in terms of design and production. Their written stories varied widely in their generic form: scientific report, video diary, (dear) diary, fairytale, spy-action movie ('My name is Blood, James Blood ...'), realist journalism ('Kate Adie reports from the front ...'), etc., all made their appearance, and led to particular selections from as well as particular configurations of the curricular content/knowledge at issue. The '(dear) diary' genre clearly demanded a quite clearly articulated episodic treatment: '8 seconds: we have just left the right ventricle ...; 15 seconds: we have delivered oxygen to the cells ...'; while the James Bond 'genre' demanded conflict, action, as well as the appearance of heroes and villains. The genre of fairytale makes yet other demands, less readily compatible with the simple structure of movement in space. However, action as movement remains central, and movement as journey remains clearly present even when it is transformed into the oppositional/antagonistic structures of the spy/action thriller genre.

Nevertheless it is clear that even within the mode of writing, the various generic possibilities have real effects on the shaping of the curricular content, and therefore on the shape of the knowledge at issue. Discourse affects choice of design, but choice of design in turn affects discourse. A genre which is well suited to narrating the rescuing of a damsel in distress ('I am Robert the Red Blood Cell') – with the settings,

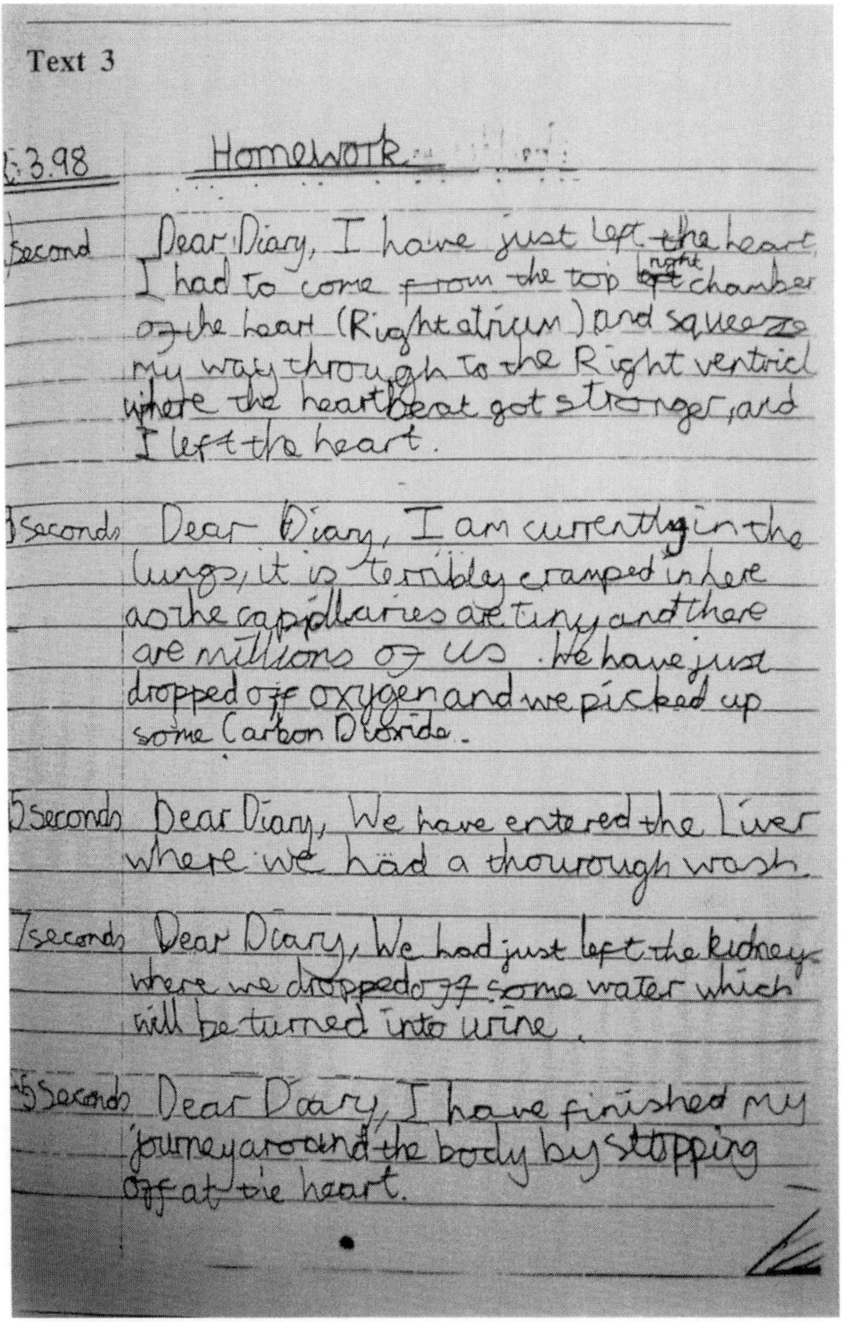

Text 3

6.3.98 Homework

1 second Dear Diary, I have just left the heart, I had to come from the top right chamber of the heart (Right atrium) and squeeze my way through to the Right ventricl where the heartbeat got stronger, and I left the heart.

3 seconds Dear Diary, I am currently in the lungs, it is terribly cramped in here as the capillaries are tiny and there are millions of us. We have just dropped off oxygen and we picked up some Carbon Dioxide.

5 seconds Dear Diary, We have entered the Liver where we had a thourough wash.

7 seconds Dear Diary, We had just left the kidney where we dropped off some water which will be turned into urine.

15 Seconds Dear Diary, I have finished my journey around the body by stopping off at the heart.

Figure 6.3 *Student's blood circulation story ('Dear Diary' genre)*

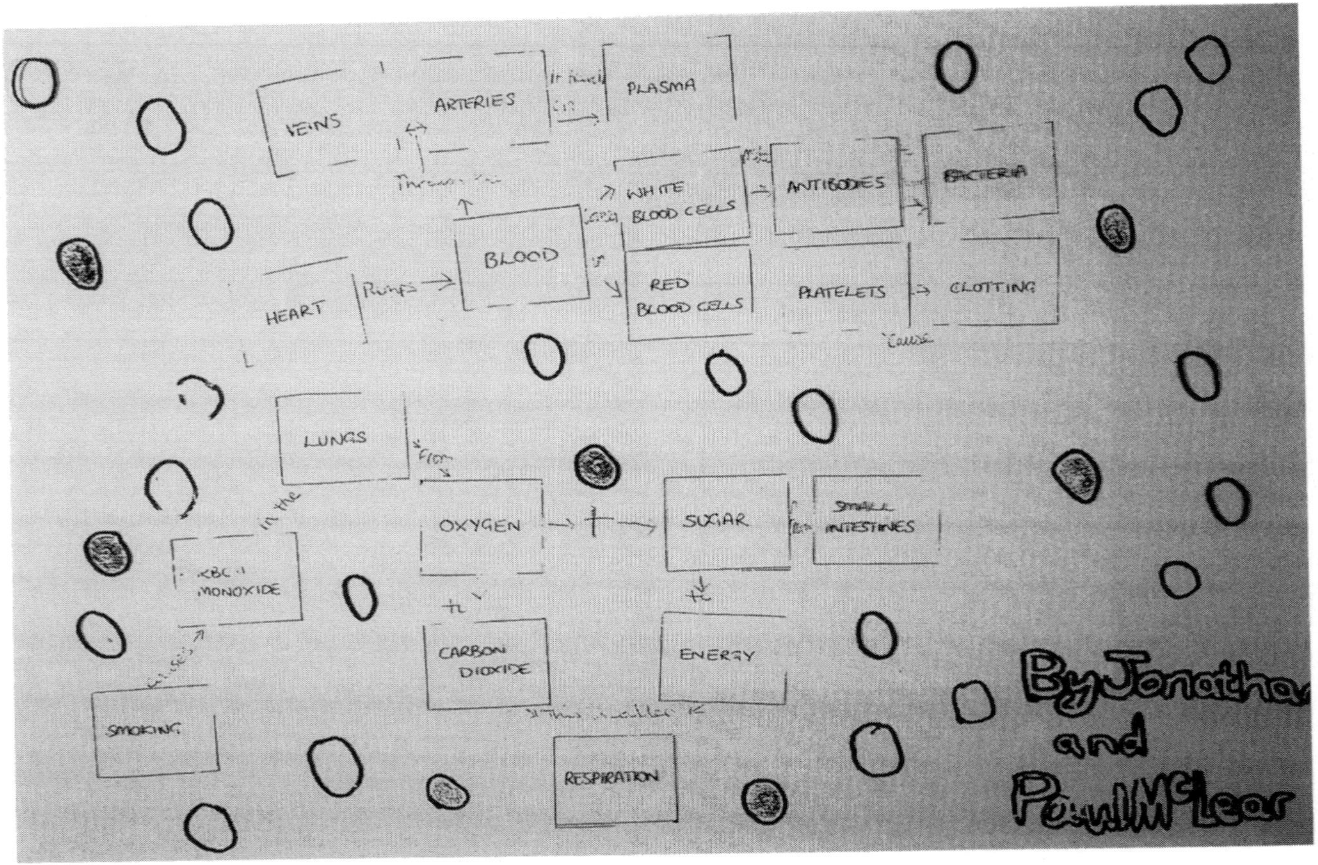

Figure 6.4 *Student's blood circulation concept map*

complications, climax, denouements required – is less well suited to an account demanding a relatively simple listing of elements. There is a requirement, for instance, for 'resolution' in the one, but not in the other; just as there is a requirement of antagonism in the spy-action thriller genre, which has no real functionality in the description of the points encountered by the red blood cell in the journey of the blood.

With concept maps there is a move to a different mode, while the topic remained that of blood *circulation*. The spatial display of the map gives rise to other possibilities. These made action less prominent or not at all present, and made action as movement in many cases a much more abstract notion, or led to action not being an issue at all. The shape of the page exerted its influence as a meaning-making resource. It suggested to many of the children that the centre of the space, for instance, could be utilised to signify 'centrality' as a semiotic concept, that is, 'centrality' as meaning 'most significant'. That then immediately posed a question (much as we pointed out above in the case of the plant-cells): what is or was most significant? The heart, as the motor that sets the whole thing in motion and keeps it going? The blood, as the central topic of the lessons? The decision to make use of the available semiotic resource of 'centre' led to a move by and large away from focus on action and movement and towards the realisation of differently, perhaps more abstractly conceived relations, realised by using the potentials both of concentric clustering around the concept chosen as central, and the meanings attached to the different quadrants of the page-space (see Kress and Van Leeuwen, 1996).

There were of course other possibilities, namely those of using the space on which the map was to be laid out as a 'page', and then as with a page making use of the possibilities of the left to right directionality of the page as it is read with the mode of writing. Movement from left to right is of course *movement*, and so action as movement could be represented in the map, though in a quite directly linear form, not open to the many variations as with the written genres. In these arrangements too the question was posed about position and placement, about what choices to make concerning the left-most ('given') and the right-most ('new') item. As with the maps organised around the semiotic resource of centrality, here too that could be answered in a number of different ways: the heart could be treated as 'given', that is, as the item which every reader would readily assume was the starting point; or heart and lungs were simultaneously represented as given (the two concepts/cards being placed one above – 'higher than' – the other, both near the middle of the left-most margin); or blood being treated as 'given'; and so on.

As with the different generic possibilities in the written mode, so here, too, mode did not fully or even narrowly determine what choices should or would be made, though mode nevertheless entered powerfully into the issue. So we might sum up here and say that however open the generic choices made by the children in their written texts left the manner of representation, the move from one mode to the other seemed to have real consequences. In the linguistic modes action as movement in various forms dominated; by contrast in the visual mode of the map, action was less in focus – other than in the linear layout of the elements, which however needed the support of written labels to make their meaning clearer.

Second, then, the question of 'control'. Our question here is about the kinds of semiotic work done, and by whom it is done. To provide a rough and ready sense of what interests us here, take the comparison between the pilgrim who experiences the narrative of the stations of the cross by walking the route laid out in some locality, pausing at each of the stations (however they are established, whether as small chapels in a cathedral, in a field, etc.), and the viewer of a Hollywood epic around the story of the life of Jesus. Both experience the narrative. Each experiences the narrative in deeply different ways, and in a deeply different manner, as an effect of the physical and semiotic work of the narrator. The question here is not one of the profundity of the experience, but of the manner, the characteristics of it, and of the differences of that experience as a result of its modal realisation. In each case there are different forms of control at issue: over the modal realisation of the narrative (the walk from cross to cross across fields on the pilgrimage, or the perception of series of shots edited into a particular sequence in the viewing of the film), over what is represented, over the potentials of apperception or of re-presentation by the experiencer of the narrative. What differences have multimodality, or the affordances of the new technologies for that matter, made in this respect?

The beholder of the mosaic on the wall of the church moves in front of the mosaic – in accord with social and cultural rules and knowledges – and the manner of the movement is coded both by the maker of the mosaic and by the social rules known to the maker and to the viewer (in its initial period of production at any rate). The reader of a written narrative moves differently: it is an internal moving, coded in the structures of the language – whether as clause, as sentence, as paragraph, as full text – and reproduced by the reader for her/himself according to the values, interests, knowledges that they bring to the narrative at the moment of reading. The control of the reader is a different kind of control from that of the beholder/viewer of the mosaic: shaped by the affordances of the mode of speech or writing, by the fact that all entities have to be presented as words, a world lexicalised, as against a world visualised and spatialised.

The questions of the structures and the possible structures arise in each case. In film the technologies of photography as well as the conventionalised practices around those technologies lead to the production of shots, in which the camera may move, the world in front of the camera may move, but in which the movements of the viewer are 'internal' movements (unlike the movements of the viewers/spectators of seventeenth- and eighteenth-century theatre, who could move while the actors on the stage also moved). New technologies – such as virtual reality representations – bring new possibilities. To the visual mode, represented in film and television as 'shot' and edited into longer units/texts, is added the possibility of unbroken movement: neither is the world segmented (whether by the structures of clause or of shot) nor the viewers' 'internal' movement limited. Such virtual reality narrative forms are now becoming commonplace in the computer games played by millions, and not only of course by children. The potentials of narrative are remade in ways which are not fully knowable at this stage. What is clear is that control (for which we have used the metaphor of 'movement') is shifting.

References

Adorno, T. (1976) *Introduction to the Sociology of Music,* New York, Seabury Press.

Adorno, T. (1978) 'On the Fetish Character in Music and the Regression of Listening', in A. Arato and E. Gebhardt, eds, *The Essential Frankfurt School Reader,* Oxford, Blackwell.

Arnheim, R. (1957) *Film as Art,* Berkeley, CA, University of California Press.

Arnheim, R. (1982) *The Power of the Center,* Berkeley, CA, University of California Press.

Barnouw, E. (1966) *A Tower in Babel: A History of Broadcasting in the United States to 1933,* New York, Oxford University Press.

Barthes, R. (1967) *Elements of Semiology,* London, Cape.

Barthes, R. (1972) *Mythologies,* London, Cape.

Barthes, R. (1977) *Image–Music–Text,* London, Fontana.

Baudrillard, J. (1996) *The System of Objects,* trans. J. Benedict, London, Verso.

Bazin, A. (1971) *What is Cinema?* Vol. II, Berkeley, CA, University of California Press.

Beck, U. (1999) *World Risk Society,* Cambridge, Polity.

Bell, A. (1991) *The Language of News Media,* Oxford, Blackwell.

Bell, P. and Van Leeuwen, T. (1994) *The Media Interview: Confession, Contest, Conversation,* Sydney, University of New South Wales Press.

Benjamin, W. (1977) *Illuminations,* London, Fontana.

Berger, J. (1972) *Ways of Seeing,* Harmondsworth, Penguin.

Berutto, M. (1999) 'Women and the Internet', M.A. dissertation, London College of Printing.

Bourdieu, P. (1986) *Distinction: A Social Critique of the Judgement of Taste,* London, Routledge.

Chanan, M. (1995) *Repeated Takes: A Short History of Recording and its Effect on Music,* London, Verso.

Chomsky, N. (1957) *Syntactic Structures,* The Hague: Mouton.

Coe, B. (1977) *The Birth of Photography,* Melbourne, Hutchinson.

Cope, B. and Kalantzis, M. (2000) *Multiliteracies,* London, Routledge.

Coulmas, F. (1989) *The Writing Systems of the World,* Oxford, Blackwell.

Crystal, D. (1969) *Prosodic Systems and Intonation in English,* Cambridge, Cambridge University Press.

Crystal, D. (1975) *The English Tone of Voice,* London, Arnold.

Durant, A. (1990) 'A New Day For Music? Digital Technologies in Contemporary Music-Making', in P. Hayward, ed., *Culture, Technology and Creativity in the Late Twentieth Century*, London, John Libbey.

Eisenstein, S. (1949) *Film Form*, New York, Harcourt Brace.

Eno, B. (1983) 'The Studio as a Compositional Tool', *Downbeat*, July: 56–7.

Fairclough, N. (1989) *Language and Power*, London, Longman.

Flint, R. (1999a) 'Towards a Semiotics for Video', unpublished paper, London College of Printing.

Flint, R. (1999b) 'Anna Gaskell – Sarah Morris', Exhibition Guide Text for exhibition by Anna Gaskell and Sarah Morris in the Museum of Modern Art, Oxford, 18 April – 27 June 1999.

Foucault, M. (1977) *The Archeology of Knowledge*, London, Tavistock.

Gardner, H. (1993) *Frames of Mind: The Theory of Multiple Intelligences*, London, Fontana.

Goffman, E. (1981) *Forms of Talk*, Oxford, Blackwell.

Goodwin, A. (1988) 'Sample and Hold: Pop Music in the Digital Age of Reproduction', *Critical Quarterly*, 30 (3): 34–49.

Halliday, M.A.K. (1967) *Intonation and Grammar in British English*, The Hague, Mouton.

Halliday, M.A.K. (1978) *Language as Social Semiotic*, London, Arnold.

Halliday, M.A.K. (1985) *An Introduction to Functional Grammar*, London, Arnold.

Hodge, R. and Kress, G.R. (1988) *Social Semiotics*, Cambridge, Polity Press.

Iedema, R. (1993) *Media Literacy Report*, Sydney, Disadvantaged Schools Project.

Jaffé, H.L.C. (1986) *De Stijl: 1917–1931, Visions of Utopia*, Oxford, Phaidon.

Katz, S. (1990) 'Plastic in the 80ies', in P. Sparke, ed., *The Plastics Age: From Modernity to Post-Modernity*, London, Victoria and Albert Museum.

Kracauer, S. (1960) *Theory of Film*, Oxford, Oxford University Press.

Kress, G.R. (1985) *Linguistic Processes in Sociocultural Practice*, Geelong, Deakin University Press; Oxford, Oxford University Press.

Kress, G.R. (1997) *Before Writing: Rethinking the Paths to Literacy*, London, Routledge.

Kress, G.R. (1998) 'On the Semiotics of Taste: Chains of Meaning', in A. Piroëlle, ed., *La représentation sociale du goût*, Dijon, PRISM.

Kress, G.R. and Van Leeuwen, T. (1996) *Reading Images: The Grammar of Visual Design*, London, Routledge.

Kress, G.R. and Van Leeuwen, T. (1998) 'The (Critical) Analysis of Newspaper Layout', in A. Bell and P. Garrett, eds, *Approaches to Media Discourse*, Oxford, Blackwell.

Kress, G.R., Jewitt, C., Ogborn, J. and Tsatsarelis, C. (2000) *Multimodal Teaching and Learning*, London, Continuum.

Kristeva, J. (1980) *Desire in Language: A Semiotic Approach to Literature and Art*, Oxford, Blackwell.

Labov, W. (1972) *Language in the Inner City*, Philadelphia, University of Philadelphia Press.

Lakoff, G. (1987) *Women, Fire, and Dangerous Things*, Chicago, University of Chicago Press.

Lakoff, G. and Johnson, M. (1980) *Metaphors We Live By*, Chicago, University of Chicago Press.

Laver, J. (1980) *The Phonetic Description of Voice Quality*, Cambridge, Cambridge University Press.

Leete-Hodge, L. (n.d.) *Mark and Mandy*, London, Peter Haddock.

Lomax, A. (1968) *Folk Song Style and Culture*, New Brunswick, NJ, Transaction Books.

McClary, S. (1991) *Feminine Endings: Music, Gender and Sexuality*, Minnesota, University of Minnesota Press.

McConnell-Ginet, S. (1977) 'Intonation in a Man's World', *Signs*, 3: 541–59.

McInnes, D. (1998) 'Attending to the Instance: Towards a Systemic Based Dynamic and Responsive Analysis of Composite Performance Text', Ph.D. thesis, University of Sydney.

McLuhan, M. (1966) *Understanding Media: The Extensions of Man*, New York, McGraw-Hill.

Malinowski, B. (1935) *Coral Gardens and their Magic*, London, Allen and Unwin.

Manzini, E. (1990) 'And of Plastic', in P. Sparke, ed., *The Plastics Age: From Modernity to Post-Modernity*, London, Victoria and Albert Museum.

Martin, C.A. (1997) 'Staging the Reality Principle: Systemic-Functional Linguistics and the Context of Theatre', Ph.D. thesis, Macquarie University, Sydney.

Martinec, R. (1996) 'Towards a Semiotics of Action', unpublished paper, London College of Printing.

Martinec, R. (1998) 'Cohesion in Action', *Semiotica*, 120 (1–2): 161–80.

Meikl, J.L. (1990) 'Plastics in the American Machine Age', in P. Sparke, ed., *The Plastics Age: From Modernity to Post-Modernity*, London, Victoria and Albert Museum.

Meilink, W. (1953) *Handboek voor de poppenspeler*, Purmerend, Muusses.

Middleton, R. (1990) *Studying Popular Music*, Milton Keynes, Open University Press.

Morris, D. (1977) *Manwatching*, London, Cape.

Morris, S. (1998) 'Operation of Gender in Online Gaming', unpublished paper, Macquarie University, Sydney.

Muthesius, S. (1982) *The English Terrace House*, New Haven and London, Yale University Press.

O'Toole, M. (1994) *The Language of Displayed Art*, Leicester, Leicester University Press.

Ong, W.J. (1982) *Orality and Literacy: The Technologizing of the Word*, London, Methuen.

Oren, T., Salomon, G., Kreitman, K. and Don, A. (1990) 'Guides: Characterizing the

Interface', in B. Laurel, ed., *The Art of Human–Computer Interface Design*, Reading, MA, Addison-Wesley.

Poynton, C. (1996) 'Giving Voice', in E. McWilliam and P. Taylor, eds, *Pedagogy, Technology and the Body*, New York, Peter Lang.

Rimbaud, A. (1960) *Oeuvres*, Paris, Editions Garnier Frères.

Roegholt. R. (1976) *Amsterdam in de 20e eeuw*, Utrecht, Uitgeverij Het Spectrum.

Sacks, O. (1984) *Seeing Voices*, Harmondsworth, Penguin.

Schafer, R.M. (1986) *The Thinking Ear*, Toronto, Arcana Editions.

Schama, S. (1987) *The Embarrassment of Riches: An Interpretation of Dutch Culture in the Golden Age*, London, Fontana Press.

Shepherd, J. (1991) *Music as Social Text*, Cambridge, Polity.

Sontag, S. (1977) *On Photography*, Harmondsworth, Penguin.

Thompson, P. and Davenport, P. (1982) *Dictionary of Visual Language*, Harmondsworth, Penguin.

Timmerman, C. (1998) 'Space as Network Transforming into Network as Space', M.A. dissertation, London College of Printing.

Van Dijk, T.A. and Kintsch, W. (1983) *Strategies of Discourse Comprehension*, New York, Academic Press.

Van Leeuwen, T. (1983) 'Roland Barthes' *Système de la Mode*', *Australian Journal of Cultural Studies*, 1 (1): 18–35.

Van Leeuwen, T. (1984) 'Impartial Speech: Observations on the Intonation of Radio Newsreaders', *Australian Journal of Cultural Studies*, 2 (1): 84–99.

Van Leeuwen, T. (1985) 'Rhythmic Structure of the Film Text', in Teun A. van Dijk, ed., *Discourse and Communication: New Approaches to the Anaysis of Mass Media Discourse and Communication*, Berlin, De Gruyter.

Van Leeuwen, T. (1987) 'Generic Strategies in Press Journalism', *Australian Review of Applied Linguistics*, 10 (2): 199–221.

Van Leeuwen, T. (1993) 'Genre and Field in Critical Discourse Analysis: A Synopsis', *Discourse and Society*, 4 (2): 193–225.

Van Leeuwen, T. (1997) 'Taste in the Framework of a Semiotics of Materiality', in A. Piroëlle, ed., *La représentation sociale du goût*, Dijon, PRISM.

Van Leeuwen, T. (1999) *Speech, Music, Sound*, London, Macmillan.

Van Leeuwen, T. and Wodak, R. (1999) 'Legitimizing Immigration Control: A Discourse-Historical Analysis', *Discourse Studies*, 1 (1): 83–119.

Virilio, P. (1997) *Open Sky*, London, Verso.

Williams, R. (1974) *Television: Technology and Cultural Form*, London, Fontana.

Williams-Jones, P. (1975) 'Afro-American Gospel Music: A Crystallization of the Black Aesthetic', *Ethnomusicology*, September: 373–85.

Winternitz, E. (1979) *Musical Instruments and Their Symbolism in Western Art*, New Haven, Yale University Press.

Index

action 42
  as semiotic 36, 40, 42
Action Man 80
adaptation 102, 103
Adorno 8
affordance 67, 125
aggregation 123
  dis- 123
analogy 77
'animated' 86
Antonioni 97
architecture
  as discourse 6
  as mode 27
Arnheim 2, 95
articulation 8, 27, 32, 49, 123
  modal 123
  multiple 4, 20
  of semiotic event 6, 40, 42
  of semiotic practice 41, 42
Art of Noise 94
assembly 102
Audio Rom 96
'author' 86

Barnouw 91
Barthes 10, 70, 71, 72, 80
Bandrillard 80, 89, 90, 96
Bazin 94
Beck 35
Bell 18
Benjamin 7, 19, 89, 91, 94
Berger 72
Berutto 108
Bourdieu 11, 71
breathiness 83

Chanan 7, 88
Chomsky 57, 113
coding 88
  re- 88
Coe 91
cohesion 57
cohesive effort 58
colligation 58
colour 27–9, 57, 63
  and discourse 25–7
  as mode 25, 32, 34, 57–8, 62–3
  as signifier 58, 59
communication 4, 8, 20, 45, 63, 71
  multimodal 123
  non-verbal 70
  by provenance 73
  situation 5
communicative practices 111, **114**
connection 2
connotation 2
Cope 46
Coulmas 90
Courlander 76
Crystal 70, 81

Davenport 112
design 4–11, 17–21, 30, 39, 45–51, 54–65, 68, 70, 86, 103, **118**, 119, 121
  and performance 7
  practices 111
  and production 6–7, 73
  schemes 120
  and semiotic event 6
  and semiotics 71
digitalisation 2
disconnection
  devices 2
  elements 2
discontinuities 3
discourse 4–11, 15, 17, 20, 21, 24, 30–6, 40, 56, 58–9, 61–8, 73, 77, 86
  ensembles of 64
  and knowledge 4
  and language 24
  and realization
discourse analysis 24
discursive action 25, 29, 30, 31, 35, 38–40, 43, 96, 111
  ensemble 61, 62, 64

distribution 4, 7, 11, 20, 86–9, 92–3, 96, 103, 121
  and digital technologies 86–92
  as language 92
  and meaning 7
  and preservation 7
  as product 103
  as semiotic 7, 11, 93
double articulation 4
  and message 4
Dual Fusion 94
Durant 96

editing 95
Eisenstein 5, 95
Epstein 77
experiential meaning potential *see* meaning potential
expression 5, 79
  and mode 79

Fairclough 30
film 2
Flint 97
'footing' 86
Foucault 30
framelines 3
framing 2, 3, 38, 42, 45
Franks 79
functional specialization 64
  and mode 64

Gardner 24
gender 81
genre 5, 35, 46, 55, 56, 60, 63, 70
Gesamtkunstwerk
  multimodal 1
Goffman 86, 87
Goodwin 96
grammar 48, 59, 60, 111, 113, 125
  and mode 3
  of design 48, 56, 59

Halliday 3, 18, 60, 70, 86
Hallidayan linguistics 4
hierarchy
  of practices 42, 43
Hodge 3, 77

Jaffe 97
Johnson 11, 75

ideology 31, 32, 34, 38
Iedema 18
image 2
integration code 2
interaction 114
interface 2
internet
  semiotic potential of 109
interpretation 8, 20, 87
  as semiotic action 40, 42
  as semiotic articulation 41
interpreters 8

Kalantzis 46
Katz 80
Kracauer 94
Kintsch 46
Kress 1, 3, 10, 17, 30, 64, 71, 77, 113, 124, 128, 131
Kristeva 70

Labov 119
Lakoff 11, 75
language 4, 6, 7, 111
  as mode 17, 18, 20, 24, **125**
Laver 81, 83
layout 60, 62
Leete-Hodge 17
Legge 7, 88
linguistics (traditional) 4, 7, 111
linguistic
  extra- 111
  para- 111
Lomax
loudness
  range 83
Love Corporation 94

Madonna 85
Malevitch 97, 101
Malinowski 69
Manzini 80, 81
Martin 3
Martinec 3, 124
materiality 24–31, 36, 58–9, 61, 67, 70, 74, 77, 80, 125
  and social practice 64
Mathieu 93
McClary 85
McConnell-Ginct 84, 85
McInnes 3
McLuhan 90
meaning 4, 68, 71–2, 122
  and fashion 71

representation and 102
interactive 102, 122
meaning potential 59
experiential 10, 11, 23, 77, **81**, 82
and signifiers 10
semiotic 23
as multimodal 77
medium 6, 7, 22, 66, 68, 79
recording 22
distribution 22
Meikl 80
Meilink 82
metaphor 11, 75
message 4, 88
Middleton 8
mode, semiotic mode 2–7, 22–37, 46, 51–67, **79**, 123
and grammar 113
and narrative 128
orchestration of 54
foregrounded 54
monomodality 1, 45, 47, 49, 51
theories of 127
Morris 109
Morris, D. 70
multimedia 103
design 103
production 43
meaning 67
multimodal
articulation 36
communication 2, 8, 11, 29, 49
ensemble 111, 112
principle 3
resource 4
texts 2, 28
multimodality 1, 11, **20**, 28, 30, 45, 47, 50, 89
and communication 111
and film 2
and design 45
and distribution 92
world of 64
loss of 89
multiple articulation 4, 20
Muthesius 37
myth 10, 72

Oldenburg 75
Ong 91, 92
oven 103, 104, 108
origination 95
O'Toole 3, 124

Newhall 95

'participation framework' 86
photography 91, 97
Poynton 84
pitch-range 83
'plastic(s)' 79, 80, 81
practice(s) 4, 23, 27
couplings of 42
preservation 93, 100, 102
media of 86–89, 93
'principal' 86
production 4, 6, 10, 111, 20–2, 41, 49, 54, 55, 66–8, 70–3, 79, 80, 86, 96, 103, 121
as organization of expression 9
and meaning 7
semiotics of 72, 74
multimedia 43
and design 69
provenance 10, 23, 27, 31, 72, 73, 79, 80, 121

reading 68
as active 68
recording 95
ethics 95
representation 4, 63, **114**
representational modes 43–5, 46
resources 4, 5, 55, 57
semiotic 111, **112**, 113
social organization of 9, 11, 27, 35, **112**
available 11, 55, 63
representational 60
rhythm 3
Rimbaud 76
Roegholt 11, 13
roughness 83

Sacks 24
scripts 7, 46, 48, 55, 56, 60, 63, 88
Schafer 89
Schama 78
Shepherd 84
semiotic 2, 9–11, 27–8, 35, 69, 70–1
social 34
semiotic
action 36, 37, 87
artefact 6
ensemble 53
environment 37
event 6
labour 88, 103
potential 87
practices 6, 35

semiotic – *contd*
  production 9, 40
  resources
  value 76
semiosis 27–8, 34, 38, 50, 77, 79
  social 34–5, 43–4
sense 27, 28
sign 10, 20, 58, 64, 69, 72–3, 111
  house as complex 40–2
  making 59, 111
signification 20, 22
signifiers 10, 58, 59
  colour as 58
  house as set of 39
  material 58–9
  and meaning potential 58–9
  mythical 73
strata 4, 9, 20, 86
  and semiotic production 9
  semiotic modes and 11
stratal configuration 9, 20
stratification
  semiotic 122
  social 11, 122
symbolism
  sound 77
  colour 77
synaesthesia 66, 67, 77
synthesis 102
syntax 10, 111

taste 71
  and meaning 71
technologies
  and mode 4
  digital 47
tension 82
text **24**
  and ideology 34
Thompson 112
Timmerman
Titian 2
transcription 102
transduction 51
transformation 36–9, 40, 51, 63–5, 95
  transformative action 38, 39, 41
  of discourse 64
translation between modes 29
transmission 100, 102

Van Dijk 46
Van Leeuwan 1, 2, 3, 8, 13, 17, 15, 18, 64, 70, 71, 82, 85, 86, 87, 113, 114, 115,124, 131
vibrate 84
Virillio 6
voice 81, 82, 83, 84, 85
  quality 81
  as semiotic resource 82

Williams 9
Williams-James 76
Winternitz 74
Wodak 13, 115
work
  as semiotic 36, 61
writing 7, 10, 62, 64, 90
  as mode 31, 128
  language as 29, 34